# The Aboriginal Population Of The San Joaquin Valley, California

*by*

S. F. Cook

# The Aboriginal Population Of The San Joaquin Valley, California
## by S. F. Cook




ISBN: 978-93-59959-04-7

Published by

## DOUBLE 9 BOOKS

2/13-B, Ansari Road
Daryaganj, New Delhi – 110002
info@double9books.com
www.double9books.com
Tel. 011-40042856

# ABOUT THE AUTHOR

S. F. Cook, the accomplished creator of "The Aboriginal Population of Alameda and Contra Costa Counties, California," stands as a high-quality determine inside the realm of historical and demographic literature. This work is frequently appeared as considered one of his masterpieces, reflecting his determination to bridging the nation-states of history and demography. With a notable pen and a profound expertise of his subjects, Cook excels in elucidating the complex historical and demographic elements of the indigenous populations in Alameda and Contra Costa Counties. His writings transcend mere data and information, facilitating a deeper connection amongst readers and fostering a superior understanding of both the past and the folks who inhabit those areas. Cook's literary prowess is a testomony to his creativity and ardour. He invitations readers on a fascinating journey thru numerous landscapes and emotions, painting vibrant pix together with his phrases. His writing style is a brilliant fusion of beauty and accessibility, making his extraordinary tales a satisfaction for readers of all backgrounds and interests. S. F. Cook's contributions to the literary global expand beyond his understanding in historical and demographic studies; his capacity to train, inspire, and connect people via the pages of his books ensures that his legacy endures as an enriching and enlightening pressure within the world of literature.

# CONTENTS

# INTRODUCTION

Ecologically the great central valley of California forms a single unit. Nevertheless it is convenient for the purposes of this paper to divide the entire area into two portions, north and south. The vast expanse from Red Bluff to the Tehachapi is too extensive to cover demographically in a single exposition. Moreover, the northern tribes, the Wintun and Maidu, are physiographically clearly segregated from the southern by the northern extension of San Francisco Bay and the delta of the rivers. Hence we shall consider here only those peoples south of the Sacramento and American River watersheds.

The area possesses definite natural limits but its exact boundaries must be to some extent arbitrary. On the north the line has already been indicated: the south bank of the upper Bay and the Sacramento River as far upstream as a point five miles below the city of Sacramento and thence easterly along the El Dorado—Amador County line into the high mountains. This follows Kroeber's tribal boundary between the Maidu and the Sierra Miwok. On the west the line starts northeast of Mt. Diablo and follows the western edge of the San Joaquin Valley to the Tehachapi Mountains. On the east we include the Sierra Nevada as far as was reached by permanent habitation on the west slope. The southern extremity is represented by the crest of the Tehachapi.

The region designated embraces the territory of the Plains and Sierra Miwok, the Yokuts, the Western Mono, the Tubatulabal, and the Kawaiisu. From the standpoint of habitat the area is diversified since it extends from the swampy valley floor through the oak country of the lower foothills into the transition life-zone of the middle altitudes. Perhaps an ecological segregation would be desirable. Such a procedure, however, would cut across tribal boundaries and make an accurate evaluation of population difficult. On the accompanying maps, areas are delineated, and numbered, primarily for convenience of reference. At the same time they conform as closely as is feasible with the natural subdivisions of the territory marked out by river valleys, lakes, plains, and mountains. It should be stressed that they do not necessarily coincide precisely with the areas occupied by specific tribes or groups of tribes.

The demography of the central valley is rendered still more complex by the fact that the contact with the white race took place in a series of steps rather than by a single overwhelming invasion. In central Mexico, or to a somewhat lesser degree in northwestern California, aboriginal life continued relatively untouched until there occurred a rapid and catastrophic occupation of the entire territory. As a result, the population was affected in a uniform manner throughout and a sufficiently clear line can be drawn between aboriginal and postcontact conditions. In the central valley the white influence was very gradual, beginning at or near the year 1770 with the entrance of the Spanish missionaries along the coast and the infiltration of a very few foreigners into the valley. The volume of invasion increased slowly over the next three decades, but the effect was intensified by the escape of numerous mission neophytes into the valley. The years after 1800 saw repeated incursions by the coastal whites who overran the floor of the valley from the Sacramento River to Buena Vista Lake. Meanwhile the foothill and mountain tribes were permitted to remain fairly intact. With discovery of gold, however, these groups lost their immunity and were rapidly destroyed. Therefore, even though we oversimplify, we may say that the aboriginal population persisted in the valley proper up to 1770, in the lower foothills up to roughly 1810, and in the higher foothills and more remote canyons of the Sierra Nevada up to 1850.

Our sources of information cover only the period during which the demographic status of the natives was undergoing change. No written record exists that describes conditions as they might have been found prior to 1770. The only possible substitute would be an examination of the habitation sites left from prehistoric times, but archaeological research in the area has not yet progressed to the point where an adequate quantitative estimate of population is available. There are three primary bodies of data to which we have access, all falling within the historical period between 1770 and 1860.

The first of these derives from the serious effort on the part of the Americans, who between 1848 and 1852 were entering the region in large numbers, to determine the quantity of natives surviving in the central valley. This task was performed by such men as Sutter, Bidwell, and Savage, together with several Indian commissioners, and army officers sent out by the government. To their reports may be added the statements contained in the local county histories published in the era of 1880 to 1890, as well as in many pioneer reminiscences.

A second major source of information consists of the ethnographic studies made within the past fifty years, among which should be mentioned the works of Kroeber, Merriam, Schenck, Gayton, and Gifford. These investigators depended principally upon informants who were elderly people in the decades from 1900 to 1940. Their memories, together with their recollection of what had been told them by their parents, carry back, on the average, to the period of the American invasion or just before it. Hence their knowledge of truly aboriginal population would be valid for the hill tribes only; yet data derived from them for that region is probably more accurate than can be obtained from the general estimates made by contemporary white men. These two types of information, contemporary American accounts and modern ethnographic material, can thus be used to supplement and check each other for the era of 1850.

For conditions in the valley before 1840 we have to depend almost exclusively upon the historical records left by the Spanish and Mexicans. These consist of a series of diaries, reports, and letters, by both laymen and ecclesiastics, together with baptism lists and censuses from the coastal missions. This array of documents is to be found in the manuscript collections of the Bancroft Library of the University of California at Berkeley.

It will be clear from these considerations that the population of the San Joaquin Valley can be determined with some degree of accuracy at two stages in the history of the region. The later period is at the point of intense occupancy by the Americans, at or near the year 1850, for here may be brought to a focus the data from both contemporary counts and the research of modern ethnographers. The earlier is for the epoch just preceding the entrance of the Spanish into California, or just before 1770. To assess the population at this period it is necessary to bring to bear information from all sources, American and Spanish, and to utilize all indirect methods of computation which may be appropriate. As a matter of historical interest, as well as to provide a background for the estimate of aboriginal population, the state of the natives in the period of the Gold Rush will be first examined.

# THE POPULATION OF
# THE SAN JOAQUIN VALLEY
# IN APPROXIMATELY 1850

## CONTEMPORARY ESTIMATES AND
## COUNTS FOR THE ENTIRE REGION

General estimates for the population of the San Joaquin Valley during the period 1848 to 1855 were made by several individuals. James D. Savage, one of the earliest settlers in the Fresno region, stated in 1851 that the population from the Tuolumne River to the Kern River was from 50,000 to 55,000. Elsewhere he modified these figures considerably (Dixon, MS, 1875) and reported the total from the Cosumnes to the Kern as 18,100, of which 14,000 were from south of the Stanislaus River. James H. Carson, another pioneer, said in 1852 that "the Indians of the Tulare Valley number nearly 6,000. About half this number inhabit the mountains.... The other portion inhabit the plains along the rivers and lakes."

In 1852 the Indian commissioner, O. M. Wozencraft, estimated for the area lying between the Yuba and the Mokelumne rivers a total of 40,000 inhabitants. He quotes old residents as saying that four years previously (i.e., in 1848) the population for the same area had been 80,000. At about the same time another agent, Adam Johnston (1853), estimated all the Sierra and valley tribes as being 80,000 strong (including both Sacramento and San Joaquin valleys). In general magnitude these figures correspond to those given by Sutter for the region bounded by the Yuba, the Stanislaus, the Sacramento, the San Joaquin, and the line of the foothills: 21,873 (Sutter, 1850). Sutter's value definitely represents conditions prior to 1847. Meanwhile H. W. Wessels reported in 1853 that from the Stanislaus south there were 7,500 to 8,000 persons. In the same year G. W. Barbour, another commissioner, referred to the reservation Indians as "seven or eight thousand hungry souls." In 1856, agent T. J. Henly put the aggregate population of the Fresno and Kings River reservations plus Tulare, Mariposa, Tuolumne, Calaveras, and San Joaquin counties as 5,150 (Henley, 1857).

It is evident that the foregoing data represent two distinctly different types of estimate: broad generalization based largely upon subjective impression and applying to the years preceding 1847, and more narrow semi-estimate derived during the years subsequent to 1849 from some attempt to make an actual count. The figures obtained from the first method are certainly too high, particularly for the period centering around 1850. On the other hand, it may be possible that the other method yielded figures which were too low.

Some check on the reliability of the estimates supplied by the various commissioners and agents may be obtained from two sources, neither of which constituted a direct attempt to assess population. These comprise reports submitted concerning (1) vaccinations and (2) distribution of blankets.

During the summer of 1851 Dr. W. M. Ryer was employed to vaccinate those Indians in the San Joaquin Valley who could be persuaded to undergo the operation. Each month Dr. Ryer submitted a voucher specifying the number of Indians vaccinated during the preceding thirty days and also mentioning the tribes and areas covered. These vouchers are included with other documents in Senate Executive Document No. 61, 32nd Congress, first session, 1852 (pp. 20 to 23). Some question might be raised concerning the accuracy of the figures, but there is no indication in the correspondence of the period of irregularity or dishonesty. Dr. Ryer claimed that he had vaccinated, from the Stanislaus to the south shore of Lake Tulare, 6,154 persons.

A somewhat smaller area was covered by four of the eighteen treaties concluded by commissioners McKee, Barbour, and Wozencraft[1] with the California tribes in 1851. These four treaties may be designated A, B, C, and N, following the order in which they are presented in the Senate Report. Under the agreements, one of the commodities which were to be furnished to the Indians by the government was blankets. The tribes included under treaties A, B, and C were to receive a total of 3,000. In treaty N (as also in several other treaties not concerned with this area) it was stated that the Indians were to receive one blanket apiece for every person over fifteen years of age, and presumably this ratio was employed universally in the issue of blankets. Under the conditions existing at that time it may safely be assumed that the persons over fifteen years of age constituted at least 80 per cent of the total population. Therefore the three treaties first mentioned (A, B, and C) must have covered 3,750 individuals. Regarding the group embraced by treaty N it is explicitly stated that "they may number ... some 2,000 to 3,000." If we take the mean, or 2,500, then the total for the area is 6,250.

The area included under the four treaties extended actually only from the Chowchilla River to the south shore of Lake Tulare and the Kern River, whereas the territory covered by Ryer during his vaccination tour began with the Stanislaus. Within the treaty limits he vaccinated 4,449 persons. The discrepancy between his total and that of the treaties poses no difficulty since it is apparent that, as would be expected with any primitive group, fewer individuals consented to be vaccinated than made known their desire to receive gifts of blankets. Hence the figure derived from potential blanket distribution is probably closer to the actuality than the vaccination figure. If, accordingly, we correct Ryer's report of 1,705 persons vaccinated north of the Chowchilla River to conform to the ratio found south of that stream, we get 2,398. If we add this to 6,250 the total is 8,648 for the entire strip from the Stanislaus to the southern end of the San Joaquin Valley.

In summarizing general estimates and counts we may discard the very high values submitted by Wozencraft, Johnston, and Sutter on the grounds that they were either mere guesses or applied to an earlier period than that which we are considering. There are left the following figures, which seem essentially valid.

| | |
|---|---|
| Ryer and the treaties (1851) | 8,648 |
| Wessels (1853) | 7,500-8,000 |
| Barbour (1853) | 7,500-8,000 |
| Henley (1856) | 5,150 |

Since the wastage of native population in the valley was exceedingly rapid during the decade of the 'fifties, these figures are remarkably consistent. As a preliminary value, therefore, based upon the best general estimates, we may set the population in 1851 at 8,600.

## ANALYSIS BASED UPON RESTRICTED AREAS

Further examination and correction are now in order. It will be noted that the estimates above do not include the area traversed by the Cosumnes, Mokelumne, and Calaveras rivers. Moreover, the federal agents confined their calculations to those natives who voluntarily or otherwise were incorporated in the local reservation system. That many Indians were overlooked, not only in the more remote foothills, but also in the valley itself cannot be doubted. In order to assess the population in greater detail as well as to introduce new sources of information it will be advantageous to break up the entire region into smaller units and consider these units one by one.

## STANISLAUS AND TUOLUMNE RIVERS

We may begin with the watersheds of the Stanislaus and Tuolumne rivers, since for this area reasonably complete information is available (see maps 1, 5, and 6, areas 7 and 9.) On May 31, 1851, the Daily Alta California reported the treaty made with tribes of this region and stated that they were 1,000 strong. This treaty (treaty E in the California Treaties) covered the courses of the two streams as far as their junction with the San Joaquin, on the one hand, and an indeterminate distance into the hills, on the other. Ryer vaccinated in the area during June of the same year and submitted a bill for 1,010 operations. He specifies 6 bands, rancherias, or tribes which were predominantly Siakumne and Taulamni, a fact which implies that he confined his attention principally to the inhabitants of the valley and the lower foothills. In the preceding discussion it was pointed out that Ryer's figures are probably too low and that a correction should be introduced. If the same ratio is used as before, the value becomes 1,420.

Adam Johnston, in a statement published in 1853 includes a map (Johnston, 1853, p. 242). Along the rivers shown on this map he has placed figures for population. According to him there were 900 Indians on the Stanislaus and 450 on the Tuolumne, or a total of 1,350. These are distinctly noted as reservation Indians and hence would not have included the entire population. Four years later, H. W. Wessels reported for the same area only 500-700 persons (Wessels, 1857). These were the Indians left on the reservations.

At about the same period, James D. Savage gave as his opinion that there were 2,500 people on the Stanislaus and 2,100 on the Tuolumne (Dixon, MS, 1875). In their report in 1853 Barbour, McKee, and Wozencraft refer to a statement by a chief named Kossus that under his jurisdiction were 4,000 persons and 30 rancherias from the Calaveras to the Stanislaus. Although these two estimates are widely at variance with those submitted by the officials, it must be remembered that both Savage and Chief Kossus may have been referring to a somewhat earlier date and that both included bands and settlements higher up the rivers than was actually reached by the commissioners. Hence, although the figure of over 4,000 is likely too high, 1,000 to 1,500 may have been too low.

With respect to the strictly lowland tribes there is but little doubt that by the year 1852 the northern Yokuts lying between Stockton and Modesto had practically disappeared. Thus the first state census, taken in 1852, showed only 275 Indians remaining on the lower Stanislaus. George H. Tinkham states that in the same year there were only 10 families (perhaps 50 persons) left from the tribe which formerly had inhabited the region between the Calaveras and the Stanislaus and had extended eastward along the latter stream as far as Knights Ferry (Tinkham, 1923). The valley plains can consequently account for no more than approximately 350 persons and it must be assumed that almost all the remaining natives were living along the border of the foothills and higher up in the mountains.

One item of some significance is the discussion of the Tuolumne River tribes by Adam Johnston, written in the year 1860, definitely after the Gold Rush period. He says there were six chiefs in command of six rancherias, the names of which he gives. These rancherias "contain from fifty to two hundred Indians, men, women and children." One of these bands, the Aplache, "resided further in the mountains," from which one may infer that the other five were also in the mountains. At an average of 125 per band, or rancheria, this means 900 people whose existence was known to Johnston as late as 1860. An equivalent number can be assumed for the Stanislaus, or 1,800 in all.

The ethnographers have given us an imposing list of villages for the area under consideration, derived entirely from modern informants. There are three of these lists, those of Kroeber (1925), Merriam[2], and Gifford,[3] which merit careful scrutiny. Kroeber's (p. 445 of the Handbook) includes 49 names, which he says are of villages "that can be both named and approximately located." Merriam's "Mewuk List" has 28 names of places located on the Stanislaus and Tuolumne. Gifford shows 49 villages which he says are "permanent," in addition to perhaps twice that number of "temporary" villages and camps. Gifford's list is probably the most carefully compiled of the three. The geographical location is indicated by counties but since his field of observation embraces Calaveras and Tuolumne counties, it coincides territorially quite exactly with the other two lists.

Certain villages are recorded by all three investigators, others by two of them, and some by only one. Concerning the existence of the first two groups there can be little, if any, doubt. Of those appearing on only one list some question might be raised. On the other hand, the care and conservatism exhibited by all three ethnographers makes it very difficult to doubt the essential validity of their data. The discrepancies are clearly due to the differences between informants and the high probability that no single informant could recall all the inhabited places over so large an area.

I have tabulated below the number of villages according to river system and according to occurrence in the lists mentioned.

|  | **Stanislaus** | **Tuolumne** |
| --- | :---: | :---: |
| Kroeber, Merriam, and Gifford | 8 | 13 |
| Kroeber and Merriam | 2 | 3 |
| Kroeber and Gifford | 6 | 5 |
| Kroeber only | 6 | 8 |

| | | |
|---|---|---|
| Gifford only | 5 | 12 |
| Merriam only | 1 | 1 |
| | — — | — — |
| Total | 28 | 42 |

We have therefore 70 reasonably well authenticated villages in the hill area traversed by the two rivers. With regard to the number of inhabitants, further data are provided by Gifford. His informant gave for each permanent place an estimate of the number of persons present in the year 1840. Gifford secured his material in approximately the year 1915 from a man very old at the time. If the informant was then seventy-five years of age, he must have been born in 1840. Hence he could scarcely be expected to remember population figures from a date much earlier than his childhood. The names and location of the villages themselves were at least semipermanent and could have been derived from the informant's parents even if not from his own memory. Hence it is probable that the figure furnished to Gifford more nearly represents the number of inhabitants in 1850 than in 1840. The average value for all 49 villages is 20.8 persons. Yet 7 villages are stated to have held 15 persons, 11 villages 10 persons, and 3 villages 5 or less persons. Such a condition argues a rapidly declining population, for no normal aboriginal settlement is likely to have contained less than 20 inhabitants. Gifford's average of 21 persons per village must, however, be accepted as representing the closest we can get to the value for the period of 1850. This means a population of 588 for the Stanislaus and 882 for the Tuolumne. The total is 1,470 for the foothill region. Between 300 and 400 may be added to account for scattered remnants along the lower courses of these rivers and on the San Joaquin itself, or 1,800 for the entire area under consideration.

To summarize, we have the following estimates for the Stanislaus-Tuolumne watershed at or about the year 1851:

| | |
|---|---|
| Savage (perhaps before 1851) | 4,600 |
| Chief Kossus | 4,000 |
| Daily Alta California, 1851 | 1,000 |
| Vaccinations by Ryer | 1,420 |
| Adam Johnston's estimate, 1853 | 1,350 |
| Adam Johnston's estimate, 1860 | 1,800 |
| H. W. Wessels, 1853 | 600 |
| Village lists | 1,800 |

The crude numerical average is about 2,070 but since the best of the above estimates, the village lists, shows no more than 1,800, it will be preferable to set 2,000 as a fair approximation.

STANISLAUS-TUOLUMNE ... 2,000

# MERCED RIVER, MARIPOSA CREEK, AND CHOWCHILLA RIVER

South of the Tuolumne are the Merced River, Mariposa Creek, and the Chowchilla River, all within the territory of the southern Miwok (see maps 1 and 4, areas 5E, 5F, 6). The earliest of the midcentury counts pertaining to the region is probably that of Savage (Dixon, MS, 1875) who put 2,100 persons on the Merced but omitted reference to any other stream between the Tuolumne and the upper San Joaquin. Ryer, in a bill submitted July 31, 1851, claimed to have vaccinated 695 persons along the Merced, principally on the lower course of that river. The value, corrected according to the system adopted previously, is 977. McKee, Barbour, and Wozencraft in a report on May 15, 1851 (Wozencraft, 1851) described the proposed reservation No. 1 between the Tuolumne and the Merced and estimated the total number of Indians on both rivers as 2,000 to 3,000, or let us say 1,250 on the Merced alone. The map of Adam Johnston, dated in early 1852, shows 500 persons on the Merced, but these were reservation Indians. The state census of 1852, as cited by the Sacramento Union for November 17, 1852, gave 4,533 persons for Mariposa County, a figure which no doubt included all the natives from the Tuolumne to the Fresno River. H. W. Wessels on August 21, 1853, wrote that there were 500 to 700 Indians on the Stanislaus and Tuolumne, 500 to 600 on the upper San Joaquin and that the entire area contained 2,500 to 3,000 (Wessels, 1857). The Merced-Fresno region therefore accounted for somewhere between 1,000 and 1,700. A rough average for all these rather haphazard estimates would be 1,000 natives on the Merced watershed and another 1,000 on the Mariposa and the Chowchilla, or 2,000 in all.

We may now turn to the village lists. Unfortunately, Gifford did not work south of the Tuolumne but we have the list given by Kroeber in the Handbook (1925) for the southern Miwok and two manuscript lists of Merriam (entitled "Mewuk Village List" and "Indian Village and Camp Sites in Yosemite Valley and Merced Canyon"). For the middle Merced Valley, from a point some ten miles below El Portal to the base of the foothills, Kroeber and Merriam both list 14 villages, to which Merriam alone adds another 10. From El Portal to a point six or seven miles downstream Merriam has found no less than 15 villages. In Yosemite Valley itself he has located 33 villages, of which 12 are qualified as either camps or summer villages, leaving 20 which he presumes are permanent. On the upper Merced, above Yosemite, and the headwaters of the Chowchilla, Kroeber has found the name of one village and Merriam one. Clearly this area has never been investigated exhaustively. For the well-known portion of the river, therefore, there are 59 located villages.

Of the 35 village sites in Yosemite and below El Portal, Merriam says 10 were large and 6 small. The rest are not qualified but were presumably medium to small. Gifford's average for the central Miwok of 21 persons per village in 1850-1852 may be applied directly, giving a population for the Merced Valley in the hills of 1,239. To this may be added, according to Ryer and to Johnston, 50 to 600 for the lower river, making a total of 1,800.

Mariposa Creek and the Chowchilla River have never been as thoroughly investigated as the Merced. Merriam's "Mewuk List" mentions 13 sites on each of the two streams, including the 6 given by Kroeber in the Handbook. At 21 persons per village this would mean a population of 273 for each or 546 for both, a value which appears rather low.

Another approach to the problem is by way of territorial comparisons. There are under consideration, including those previously discussed, five small river systems, those of the Stanislaus, Tuolumne, Merced, Mariposa, and Chowchilla. Physiographically and ecologically they are very similar since the rivers all descend the foothills of the Sierra Nevada and traverse the plain to the San Joaquin through the same life zones and at nearly the same latitude. There are, to be sure, some local differences between them with respect to how much of their course is favorable for village sites, but in the aggregate the similarities outweigh the differences. It is of interest, therefore, to estimate the village density along each watercourse. This value can be computed with a fair degree of accuracy by measuring on a large-scale map the length of each river and its principal affluents from the edge of the plain to the upper limit of known permanent habitation. The village numbers can be derived from the lists of Kroeber, Gifford, and Merriam.

| River | Estimated Length (mi.) | Villages | Villages per river mi. |
|---|---|---|---|
| Stanislaus | 85 | 28 | 0.33 |
| Tuolumne | 105 | 42 | 0.40 |
| Merced | 125 | 59 | 0.47 |
| Mariposa | 40 | 13 | 0.32 |
| Chowchilla | 65 | 13 | 0.20 |
| Mean | | | 0.34 |

The figures, considering physiographic differences and varying coverage by ethnographers, are quite consistent. Only that for the Chowchilla appears unduly low and this in turn may be referable to an incomplete count by Merriam. It is reasonable to concede this possibility and assume an actual count of 0.30 village for each mile of this stream. On 65 miles of river front there would thus have been 19.5 villages. This consequently means, using Gifford's population average of 21 per village, 273 inhabitants on the Mariposa and 410 on the Chowchilla. These may be added to the 1,800 calculated for the Merced, making a total of 2,483.

The very approximate value derived from general estimates was 2,000 persons. The village data are probably more accurate and may be rounded off to an even 2,500.

MERCED-MARIPOSA-CHOWCHILLA ... 2,500

## THE COSUMNES, MOKELUMNE, AND CALAVERAS RIVERS

The northern Miwok held the upper reaches of the Mokelumne plus most of the Cosumnes and Calaveras (see maps 1, 5, and 6, areas 10, 11, 12). The population must have been very small in the period of the early 1850's owing to extreme attrition suffered from the Spanish and particularly from the gold miners. Kroeber gives only 20 villages on all three streams, most of them on the Mokelumne. Merriam adds another 3, making 23 in all. At Gifford's population value this means 480 persons. The official sources are of little help since none of the agents or commissioners reported specifically on the area. Evidently there were too few survivors among the natives to warrant the trouble of placing them under the reservation system.

Savage assessed the population on the Cosumnes, Mokelumne, and Calaveras at 1,000 each (Dixon, MS, 1875) but it is likely that he was thinking in terms of the days before the Gold Rush. F. T. Gilbert (1879, p. 113) says that the Mokelkos, by which he means all the Indians between the Mokelumne and the Cosumnes in the hills and as far as Stockton on the plain, had 12 rancherias of 200 to 300 each and numbered about 3,000 in all. He, however, was referring specifically to the period "before the advent of Sutter." Likewise J. D. Mason (1881, p. 256) ascribed to the same tribe "nearly a score of towns, with a total of 3,000 to 4,000." In amplification Gilbert says that in 1850 rancherias lined both banks of the Mokelumne from Ahearn's (near Lodi) to Campo Seco (near the present Pardee Reservoir), and that they numbered then about 2,000. In 1852, however, there were only 4 rancherias left, with 390 inhabitants.

Gilbert was referring explicitly to the lower course of the rivers, whereas the villages cited by Kroeber were definitely above this region in the foothills. We may accept Gilbert's figure of 390 on the lower Mokelumne, to which may be added 110 for the lower Cosumnes and Calaveras and 480 for the upper villages, making a total of 980 or, let us say, 1,000.

COSUMNES-MOKELUMNE-CALAVERAS ... 1,000

## THE FRESNO AND THE UPPER SAN JOAQUIN RIVERS

We next turn south and consider the valleys of the Fresno and upper San Joaquin rivers (see maps 1 and 4, areas 5B, 5C, 5D.) There are three counts or estimates pertaining to this area specifically. The first is that of Savage, who does not mention the Fresno but puts 2,700 persons on the upper San Joaquin. The second source is the May 29, 1851, issue of the Daily Alta California, which carried a letter written by an unidentified officer who was with the Indian commissioners and in fact may have been G. W. Barbour. This officer refers to the treaty made with the natives between the Chowchilla and the Kings rivers and says that "the total is probably 3,000 Indians." The third is Adam Johnston, who on his map ascribed 1,200 people to the Fresno and 1,000 to the San Joaquin (Johnston, 1853). The average of the three estimates is 2,633.

W. M. Ryer submitted three reports for the territory below the Merced and north of the Tehachapi Mountains. In each he mentions the tribes vaccinated (Ryer, 1852). There are 45 in all, but 8 tribal or rancheria names are indeterminate and there are many duplicate names among the rest. Putting all three lists together we can get 27 recognizable tribal names, of which one is southern Miwok, four are Mono, and the others Yokuts. The total vaccinations performed numbered 4,451, or, correcting to conform to the figures based on blanket distribution, 6,255, an average of 232 per tribe. To allow for the nontribal and unrecognizable names on Ryer's lists this value may be arbitrarily reduced to 200. Ryer mentions in the Fresno-San Joaquin area the following: Chowchilla, Chukchansi, Heuchi, Pitkachi, Goshowu, Dumna, Dalinchi, Pohinichi (Miwok), and Posgisa (Mono). The Pohinichi should be excluded since they have already been considered in connection with the southern Miwok. The other nine, reckoned at 200 persons per tribe, would represent an aggregate of 1,800. However, Kroeber (1925, p. 481, and map, p. 526) shows four other Yokuts subdivisions within the same territory: Hoyima, Wakichi, Kechayi, and Tolichi. Although Ryer may have included these under other tribal names they perhaps ought to be included here, thus making the total 2,600.

For villages there are two sets of sources. The first pertains primarily to the Yokuts, covers a territory substantially coterminous with that seen by the contemporary observers mentioned above, and is found in the work of

Kroeber (1925), Gayton (1948), and Latta (1949). The second set of villages is confined to the Mono and is derived from Gifford (1932) and Merriam.

The first group of authors list villages for the 13 tribes mentioned in the preceding discussion, 49 in all or an average of 3.77 per tribe. With respect to size there is reason to believe that the settlements in this area, even in the early 1850's, were considerably larger than those described by Gifford for the central Miwok. The estimate of Adam Johnston of an average of 125 per rancheria on the lower Tuolumne has already been mentioned. H. W. Wessels in 1853 wrote that the Pitkachi plus the Noo-to-ah, a Mono group, had 500 to 600 souls (Wessels, 1857). Half of these, or 300, may have been Pitkachi, a tribe for which Kroeber lists 3 villages. This would have meant 100 per village. Merriam credits Savage with the statement that in 1851 the Kechayi had 1,000 people. Kroeber, Gayton, and Latta list 6 different villages for this tribe or, according to Savage's figures, 167 persons per village. Ryer's total of 2,600 prorated among 49 villages, would yield 53 persons each. Although it is probable that the values computed from the statements of Johnston, Wessels, and Savage are too high, that derived from Ryer may be somewhat too low. An intermediate figure of 70 inhabitants per village for the valley and lower foothills would perhaps come as close as we can get to the truth. This, with 49 villages, gives 3,430, somewhat more than the 2,633 cited as the average of the general estimates.

Inhabiting the higher foothills and extending to the upper limit of habitation from the San Joaquin to the Kaweah rivers were the Western Mono. This tribe lived just above the Yokuts and at points was in very close association with them. As a whole the Western Mono constitute a racial and ecological unit and as such it is probably preferable to consider them as a single population entity than to segregate them by rivers, as has been done for the Miwok and the Yokuts. It will be necessary, therefore, to digress for this purpose and subsequently return to the discussion.

The classic ethnographic work on the tribe, and the only work which contains any numerical data, is that of Gifford (1932) on the North Fork division of the Mono. This is supplemented by Merriam's manuscript entitled "Monache Tribes, Bands, and Villages." Gifford gives the names (text and map) of 67 North Fork villages, or, as he prefers to call them, hamlets. These were quite unlike either those of the Miwok or of the valley Yokuts, being very much smaller and subject to an extraordinary turnover in inhabitants. Gifford makes it very clear that each family was accustomed to move every few years from one settlement to another and that sites were being continually occupied and deserted. The 67 names are therefore no criterion for population. For the time of the American occupation Gifford estimates the number of persons in the group or subtribe as approximately

300, which, divided directly by 67, would give the absurd average of 4 persons per hamlet. However, a more detailed analysis is possible.

Of Gifford's 67 names, 2 may be deducted as being only camps, leaving 65 which at some period were permanently occupied. In his Appendix A (pp. 57-61) he lists the sites, together with the number of houses in each and the number of males and females inhabiting them. From these data may be computed the total number of families and the mean number of persons per family. There were 227 families in all. However, 36 of these are listed two or more times by virtue of moves made from one hamlet to another, which were remembered by Gifford's informants. This would leave 191 families for the subtribe, provided Gifford recorded all the moves. But Gifford clearly implies that he did not, since his informants could not remember them all. Hence the number of families must be further corrected. In Appendix A, 15 out of a total of 65 hamlets were concerned in the moves recorded. These 15 hamlets were inhabited at different times by 61 families but many of these, owing to frequent change of residence, are repetitions. Actually there was a total of 24 different families rotating among the 15 villages. Now if in the other 50 hamlets the same process was going on, although Gifford was not able to record the moves, it is legitimate to apply the same ratio as is in fact found for the 15 hamlets. The crude total of 227 families must therefore be reduced to 89. From Gifford's complete list it can be determined that there were on the average 4.93 persons per family. This gives a population of 439 for the period remembered by the informants.

On general grounds it is to be expected that the conditions reported by Gifford's informants were not entirely aboriginal. This is also indicated by the value of 4.93 persons per family, which is somewhat too low for a stable prehistoric population. Moreover, Gifford himself states that there were formerly 44 more houses than there were in the time referred to by the informants (figures given individually for the hamlets in App. A). About 1850 there were 227 houses, and if 44 are added, the aboriginal number would have been 271. Each house may be assumed to have held one family but the houses were probably occupied in rotation. The crude estimate of 271 houses or families, each containing (according to aboriginal standards) a possible 6 persons, would mean a total of 1,626 for the subtribe. If, however, we apply the correction factor for family moves we must reduce this estimate to 640, a far more reasonable figure. For the North Fork Mono, therefore, we may accept as the best estimate obtainable a population of 440 for the period near 1850 and of 640 for precontact time.

The other subtribes of the Mono provide no data comparable with those available for the North Fork group. Some method of extrapolation is thus called for.

The village method is very unsatisfactory. Kroeber says substantially nothing on this score and Merriam, although he lists 19 villages for the North Fork Mono, gives no more than one or two or, at the most, half-a-dozen names for each of the other groups. Tribal distinctions are also very confusing. Kroeber in the Handbook mentions 6 Mono subtribes: North Fork group, Posgisa, Holkoma, Wobonuch, Waksachi, and Balwisha. Merriam subdivides to a much greater extent. His grouping may be expressed essentially as follows:

| | | |
|---|---|---|
| 1. Pogesas | equivalent to Kroeber's Posgisa |
| 2. Nim | synonymous with the North Fork subtribe |
| 3. Kwetah | included in Kroeber's Holkoma |
| 4. Kokoheba | included in Kroeber's Holkoma |
| 5. Holkoma | included in Kroeber's Holkoma |
| 6. Towincheba | included in Kroeber's Holkoma |
| 7. Toinetche | included in Kroeber's Holkoma |
| 8. Tsooeawatah | included in Kroeber's Holkoma |
| 9. Emtimbitch | classed by Kroeber as a Yokuts tribe |
| 10. Woponuch | equivalent to Kroeber's Wobonuch |
| 11. Wuksatche | equivalent to Kroeber's Waksachi |
| 12. Padoosha | equivalent to Kroeber's Balwisha |

Nos. 5 to 8 inclusive are consolidated by Merriam as smaller groups within a main group or subtribe called the Toohookmutch. Concerning these Merriam says: "Large tribe on King's River. On both sides but largest area on north side. Contains many rancheria bands."

Using Merriam's nomenclature, the Nim are generally conceded to have been the largest single subtribe. For this we may take as a working base line the previous estimate of 440 persons and Merriam's list of 19 villages. Elsewhere Merriam mentions the names of the following: Toinetche 3 villages, Holkoma 4, Woponuch 9, Emtimbitch 2, Waksache 1, Kokoheba 1, and Toohookmutch 10. The total is 30. By direct proportion the inhabitants should have numbered 695 but this would leave five of Merriam's groups with no population at all. If we consider that the Toohookmutch complex plus the Kokoheba and Kwetah are the equivalent of Kroeber's Holkoma we find 18 villages, which implies 416 people. Merriam cites 9 villages or, at the same ratio, 208 persons for the Wobonuch. The total for these three of Kroeber's subtribes would then be 1,064. If we guess that the remaining groups contained 500 persons, the figure for the Mono in 1850 would reach the vicinity of 1,600.

In view of the paucity of the village data for all subtribes except the North Fork group it is proper to fall back on area-density comparisons. The territory actually inhabited by the Mono is vague, particularly on the eastern border approaching the high mountains. Nevertheless Merriam's villages furnish a fair guide in outline, since his findings, while very incomplete, can be regarded as a reasonably well distributed sample. Moreover, his descriptions of tribal boundaries and village locations appear to be very accurate. When we plot the latter on a large scale map, therefore, the outlines of the Western Mono area become sufficiently distinct.

There are two possible variants of the method, one by computing stream distances and the other by measuring areas. Both must of course rest for their basis on the data for the North Fork subtribe. This in turn may entail some error, since the North Fork group may have been not only the most populous but also the densest.

For the North Fork territory the distribution shown by Gifford on his map (1932, p. 18) is used plus the area of Bass Lake, since Merriam has found that there were once villages there. The southern and eastern boundary is taken as the San Joaquin River, because the North Fork Mono apparently did not cross to the left bank of the river. Several miles on Little Fine Gold Creek must also be included, according to Gifford's map.

In this region there were approximately 60 miles of streams, including the San Joaquin River itself. With a population of 440 this means 7.33 persons per stream mile. The stream mileage for the San Joaquin system as a whole within the Mono boundaries amounted to 100 miles. Hence the population in the same ratio would be 733. The analogous values for the Kings River system are 150 miles and 1,100 persons and for the Kaweah drainage 75 miles and 550 persons. The total population would then be 2,383.

If areas are calculated from the township lines on the map, that covered by the North Fork Mono is approximately 150 square miles and that of the Mono collectively is 1,090 square miles. Equating the North Fork population to the entire area gives for the Mono as a whole 3,195.

We may now return to the consideration of the Fresno-San Joaquin region. For the lower courses of these rivers, mainly in Yokuts territory, three values were derived, 2,633 from general estimates, 2,600 from Ryer's vaccinations, and 3,430 from village lists. We may accept the average, 2,890.

For the Mono of the upper San Joaquin the best estimate, as given above, is 733. The total is 3,623 or, rounded off to the nearest hundred, 3,600.

FRESNO-SAN JOAQUIN ... 3,600

## THE KINGS AND THE KAWEAH RIVERS

The Kings and Kaweah watersheds may be considered at this point in their entirety (see maps 1 and 3, areas 3 and 4). If we deduct 730 persons for the San Joaquin basin, the estimates for the Mono on the two former streams was estimated by the village method as 870, by the stream mileage method as 1,653, and by the area method as 2,465. If one regards some of these figures as too high, he should bear in mind that the natives on the Kings and Kaweah rivers were exposed to more intense contact with the white race for a longer period before 1850 than those on the relatively sheltered North Fork, and that their extermination proceeded with tremendous velocity after that date. This fact may well account for the inability of either Kroeber or Merriam to find more than a few villages on the Kings and Kaweah, as compared with the success of Gifford on the North Fork. The more exposed villages may simply have disappeared before the era reached by the memory of modern informants. If this is so, the stream mileage and area comparisons may be more accurate than otherwise might be supposed.

Considerable evidence for a rather high population in this region at the midpoint of the nineteenth century is to be derived from contemporary accounts and from statements obtained by Merriam. Among the papers in his collection is a clipping from the Stockton Record of February 21, 1925, containing an article by Walter Fry of the United States Park Service. Included is an account of early days on the Kaweah by Hale D. Thorpe, obtained by Mr. Fry in 1910. Mr. Thorpe says:

> When I first came to the Three Rivers country in 1856, there were over 2,000 Indians living along the Kaweah River above Lemon Cove. Their headquarters camp was at Hospital Rock.... There were over 600 Indians then living at the camp.

The Indians were mostly Mono, of the Patwisha tribe. Dr. Merriam evidently consulted Mr. George W. Stewart concerning this matter, since the file also contains a letter from Mr. Stewart written to Dr. Merriam on March 29, 1926, stating that this camp was occupied only during the summer and that there were several permanent rancherias along the stream. Mr. Thorpe's figure of 2,000 probably refers to Indians of all tribes, since by 1856 all the natives from the delta region had been driven up the river. The 600 at or near Hospital Rock were undoubtedly Mono.

In his manuscript entitled "Ho-lo-ko-ma, Cole Spring, Pine Ridge," Merriam has the following to say:

> Ben Hancock, who has lived in this country about 40 years [in 1903] tells me that when he came here there were about 500 Indians (Ko-ko-he-ba) living in Burr Valley, a few on Sycamore Creek, 600 or 700 at Cole Spring (Hol-ko-mahs) and about the same number (also Hol-ko-mahs) in Fandango Ground and in Haslet Basin.... He says a very large village was stretched along the south side of King's River two or four miles below the mouth of Mill Creek and for half a mile the dome grass-covered houses nearly touched. There were also large villages on Dry Creek and one above the forks of King's River some miles above Dry Creek. The tribe at the forks is now extinct."

(There is only one survivor of the Burr Valley tribe.)

Although the numbers may be somewhat exaggerated, there is no reason why the essential correctness of this account should be questioned. This is particularly true in view of the circumstantial detail with which it is recorded. The Kokoheba must be regarded as having a population of at least 500 and the Holkoma of 1,200, making 1,700 for the Kings River Mono. If there were 730 on the upper San Joaquin and 600 on the upper Kaweah and if 500 are added for the Emtimbitch-Wobonuch group, the total is 3,530, not much more than was calculated by means of area comparisons.

For the Kings River as a whole the estimates of 1850 to 1853 indicate a substantial Indian population. Savage (Dixon, MS, 1875) sets the number as 2,000, a remarkably low figure for him. G. W. Barbour and Adam Johnston (Sen. Ex. Doc. 4, 1853, pp. 253-256) both state that for the purpose of consummating treaties 4,000 Indians came to Camp Belt on the Kings River in 1851. Lt. George H. Derby in his careful account of the southern part of the central valley in 1851 says that there were 17 rancherias on Kings River, "numbering in all about three thousand including those situated among the hills in the vicinity" (Derby, 1852). Many of these were Choinimni, but at least half must have been Mono.

If we accept Derby's count of 17 villages for 3,000 persons, the average number of inhabitants per rancheria would be 177. For the area farther north the equivalent number was taken as 70. There is reason to believe that for the basins of the Kings and Kaweah Derby's figure of 177 is a closer approximation. Ben Hancock's description of the village on the Kings below Mill Creek is very graphic and explicit (see citation above.) If the "dome-grass covered houses nearly touched" and stretched along the river in only a single row, and if each occupied 50 linear feet, then there must have been 52 houses in half a mile. Allowing 5 persons per house, in accordance with Gifford's data for the North Fork Mono, the inhabitants must have numbered 260. One of the rancherias seen by Derby was Cho-e-mime which had 70 "warriors." Reckoning the "warriors" as half the males the population would have been 280. Derby says the village of Notonto (of the tribe Nutunutu on the south bank of the lower Kings) had 300 inhabitants. These places were of course relatively large and important and do not represent the general average. However, the village of Notonto must have reached fully 150 persons.

Apart from the Mono, the tribes located on the Kings River were all Yokuts, as follows: Aiticha, Apiachi, Wimilchi, Nutunutu, Wechihit, Toihichi, Chukomina, and Choinimni. For these the modern ethnographers Kroeber, Gayton, Latta, and Stewart have been able to locate and identify 25 villages inhabited during the youth of informants. Since this covers a somewhat larger territory than was seen by Derby, the correspondence in number of rancherias is reasonably close. At 150 persons per village the population would be 3,750. If we add 1,700 for the Kings River Mono, the total is 5,450. However, there may have been some overlap, so this figure may be reduced to 5,000. It should be noted that the area embraced within this estimate includes the Kings River basin as a whole, together with that of all its affluents.

The Kaweah River from Lemon Cove to the town of Tulare diverges to form a delta, which originally contained a very large native population. At the time of the American occupation there had occurred a material reduction, which was accelerated by the fact that the region provided excellent farming land for the entering Americans. Hence the value for the population in 1850-1853 must be relatively low in comparison with preceding decades. In May, 1851, according to G. W. Barbour (1853, pp. 253-255) there were 7 tribes on the Kaweah, and 1,200 people came to treat with the commissioners. These tribes included the following: Chunut, Choinok, Wolasi, Telamni, Gawia, Yokod, and Wukchamni. Of these, the first, the Chunut, inhabited the shore of Lake Tulare and should not be included as a Kaweah River tribe. The estimated population of the remainder would, therefore, be approximately 1,000, if the figure of the commissioners is to be taken without qualification.

With respect to the individual tribes there are a few scattered bits of information. Derby (1852) mentions three rancherias or bands in the area: Cowees (Gawia) with 200 people, Thulime (Telamni) with 65 men, or roughly 200 people, and Heame-a-tahs (Telamni) with 200 people. Merriam in his "Yokuts List" cites an informant who said that the Wukchumne "used to number" 5,000 and occupied the valley now called Lemon Cove and up and down the Kaweah River. Clearly this is an extreme overestimate, unless the informant was referring to the period prior to 1800. Finally Merriam cites a letter by Lt. N. H. McLean, which states that the "Four Creeks Country" included the "Cahwiahs, Okuls, Choinux, Wicktrumnees, Talumnies" and in 1853 had not over 1,200 souls.[4]

It thus appears quite evident that the six Yokuts tribes, except perhaps the Wukchumni, had no more than 200 persons apiece during the era under consideration. From modern informants Kroeber, Gayton, and Latta have obtained for the Choinok, Gawia, Telamni, Yokod, and Wolasi collectively the names of only 8 villages. Assuming the Kings River value of 150 persons per village, which seems to be confirmed by Derby for the Kaweah River also, this means 1,200 persons for the five tribes. Gayton and Latta, however, find 15 names for the Wukchumni, which would indicate a population of 2,250. Such a figure is highly unlikely. It is probable that earlier times are referred to by the informants or that there is confusion among tribal affinities. Alternatively, the Wukchumni villages may have followed the style of the hill-dwelling Mono and have been very much smaller than has been indicated by Derby for the valley-inhabiting Yokuts. Since we cannot resolve the difficulty with the data at hand, it is better to accept the practically unanimous opinion of contemporary white observers that the population below Lemon Cove did not exceed 1,200 in 1851. To these must be added the 600 Mono previously discussed, making a total for the Kaweah River as a whole of 1,800 persons.

If the two river basins are considered jointly, the method of area comparisons as applied to the Mono, estimates by government officials, accounts by early pioneers, and the village lists secured from modern informants all apparently agree that the population of the region reached several thousand as late as 1850 and 1851. We may therefore accept the total of 6,800, or 5,000 on the Kings and 1,800 on the Kaweah.

KINGS-KAWEAH ... 6,800

## THE TULARE LAKE BASIN

The shores of Tulare Lake (see maps 1 and 2, area 2) were aboriginally inhabited by three tribes, the Tachi, Wowol, and Chunut. In close proximity on the northeast were the Nutunutu, but since the latter have been included with the Kaweah River tribal group, they must be omitted from consideration here. Savage allocated 1,000 Indians to Tulare Lake (Dixon, MS, 1875). McLean said there were 1,000 Indians "on the lakes" in 1853, 500 of which were "Notontos," leaving 500 for the "Taches" and "Tontaches" (Merriam collection). The most reliable account is that of Derby (1852).

However, Derby in his terminology confused the Tachi with the Chunut, in which mistake he has been followed by Merriam (under title "Indians of the Tache Lake Region in 1850," MS). Derby makes it clear in his account that he found the village of Sintache (population 100) at the northern side of the then nearly dry Lake Tontache, that is to say on the southern shore of the big Lake Tache (Tulare). These were probably Chunut. There was also a small rancheria which he called Tinte-Tache at the south side of the same lake, i.e., Tontache (population 50). These are likely to have been Wowol. The tribe known to ethnographers as the Tachi were north of the big lake (i.e., Lake Tache or Tulare). Their chief told Derby that they had 800 people and that their principal rancheria was northwest of the lake (population 300). Since Derby also applies the name of Tinte-Tache to the northwest village, it is clear that there were two rancherias of this name included in his account.

Kroeber and Gayton mention a total of 8 villages for the Tachi. If one of these had 300 people, as Derby states, then the average population of the other seven was approximately 70. This agrees with Derby's two southern rancherias of 50 and 100 persons respectively. For the Chunut Kroeber, Gayton, and Latta all mention the village of Chuntau. Kroeber mentions one other, Miketsiu. This would indicate a population of nearly 150. For the Wowol the ethnographers give three villages, or an implied population of, say, 220. The total for the lakes would then reach 1,170, or very close to the general contemporary estimate of 1,000. The figure 1,100 may be accepted as a compromise.

TULARE LAKE BASIN ... 1,100

## TULE RIVER, KERN RIVER, AND THE BUENAVISTA BASIN

The remaining Yokuts territory is large in area but relatively small in population. It includes the watersheds of the Tule and Kern rivers together with those of the small creeks between (Deer, White, and Poso creeks) and Buenavista Basin south of Bakersfield (see maps 1 and 2, areas 1F and 1G). The tribes placed by Kroeber in the region are the Koyeti, Yaudanchi, Bokninuwad, Kumachisi, Bankalachi (Shoshonean), Paleuyami, Yauelmani, Hometwoli, Tuhohi, and Tulamni.

G. W. Barbour (1852), in a letter dated July 28, 1851, said that the area bounded by Buenavista Lake, Tule River, and Paint Creek contained a population of about 2,000. Savage (Dixon, MS, 1875) said there were 1,700 on the Kern River and Barbour (1853) stated that, for treaty-making purposes in 1851, 1,700 congregated at Paint Creek below Tule River. The villages listed by Kroeber, Gayton, and Latta for the various tribes are as follows: Bokninuwad 2, Hometwoli 3, Koyeti 8, Kumachisi 6, Paleuyami 7, Tuhohi

1, Tulamni 3, Yaudanchi 8, and Yauelmani 7. The total is 45. The village size indicated by Derby for the Tulare Lake Basin and adjacent valley territory is 60 or 70; that for the hill regions is undoubtedly smaller. If we take 40 persons as the average village population, the aggregate for the region would be 1,800 and if we take 50 persons, it is 2,250. We cannot be far in error in setting the population at Barbour's value, 2,000.

TULE-KERN-BUENAVISTA ... 2,000

On the basis of gross estimates and semicomprehensive counts for the entire region the population for the San Joaquin Valley and neighboring foothills in 1851 was tentatively set at 8,600 (p. 34). The detailed consideration of the seven subdivisions of the entire region, as above, leads to an estimate of 19,000, as set forth in the following recapitulation.

| | |
|---|---|
| Stanislaus-Tuolumne | 2,000 |
| Merced-Mariposa-Chowchilla | 2,500 |
| Cosumnes-Mokelumne-Calaveras | 1,000 |
| Fresno-San Joaquin | 3,600 |
| Kings-Kaweah | 6,800 |
| Tulare Lake Basin | 1,100 |
| Tule-Kern-Buenavista | 2,000 |
| Total | 19,000 |

It is believed that this total is more reliable than that previously given for several reasons. In the first place, it is derived from a careful consideration of all available sources in detail. In the second place, the preliminary estimate was weighted heavily by the reports of government officials, who saw principally those Indians with whom they were able to make treaties or whom they were able to collect on reservations. That this seems to represent less than one-half the natives in the territory is not surprising. In the third place, recent investigations by ethnographers have brought to light many local groups which were overlooked by contemporary observers, official and civilian alike. We may therefore accept the figure 19,000 as the population of the San Joaquin Valley surviving in 1852.

## FOOTNOTES:

[1] These treaties seem to have been concluded without proper authorization from the Federal government and were never ratified by the Senate. They were incorporated in Senate Confidential Documents, June, 1852, and remained

unpublished for half a century. Finally they were ordered printed in 1905 as a Senate Reprint and are now available under the title of "18 California Treaties."

[2] This village list and all others herein referred to under the name of Merriam are part of the extensive file of personal manuscript material collected by the late C. Hart Merriam and deposited, through the kindness of his heirs, with the Department of Anthropology of the University of California, Berkeley. Merriam's village lists were very carefully compiled and for many regions of the state cannot be duplicated in any publications which have hitherto appeared.

[3] I am indebted to Professor Edward W. Gifford, of the Department of Anthropology of the University of California, Berkeley, for the privilege of examining his list of Central Miwok villages, which was obtained some years ago through an informant and has remained unpublished.

[4] Merriam's manuscript entitled "Yokuts List" mentions a report from Lt. N. H. McLean, dated July 12, 1853, to H. J. Wessels, on file in "Old Files Division," Adjutant General's Office, Washington, no. H369. As far as I am aware, this letter has never been quoted elsewhere.

# THE ABORIGINAL POPULATION

In order to estimate the aboriginal population of the San Joaquin Valley it is necessary to rely very heavily on the accounts furnished by the colonial Spanish and Mexicans. These were primarily ecclesiastics and military men who entered the territory for purposes of exploration, to seek new converts to the missions, or to chastise stock raiders. The more responsible of these left circumstantial and, as a rule, fairly accurate narratives and diaries. Unless there is in a particular case some reason for doubt, their statements may be accorded considerable confidence.

At the same time two circumstances often render the interpretation of the data derived from these documents difficult. The first is the lack of consistent designations for places. During the process of opening up the area it was inevitable that rivers and villages should be assigned different names by one explorer after another and that the same name should be applied to more than one locality. The second is that during the early phases of exploration some localities were visited repeatedly, whereas others were overlooked perhaps entirely. Hence the information available to us is very uneven; it permits us to achieve a reasonably clear idea of the population of one region but leaves another almost completely blank. As a result extrapolation by area is almost unavoidable.

It must also be constantly borne in mind that the Spanish records themselves do not give us an absolutely undistorted picture of aboriginal conditions. It is very evident from the reports of the earliest official pioneers, like Garcés in 1776 and Martin in 1804, that from 1770 onward and perhaps even before white men had straggled into the valley and had consorted with the natives. There is reason to believe that these unknown interlopers may have introduced diseases which adversely affected the population and may have initiated a process of general social disruption. The best we can do is get as close to the prehistoric condition as the records allow.

Two other demographic consequences arise from this very early white contact. In the first place, the documentary record, if we ignore Garcés for the moment, runs nearly continuously from 1804 to approximately 1840. During this long period an uninterrupted change was going on among the native population: the population was continually decreasing. Hence later reports tend to deviate from earlier ones, and indeed may show an entirely new state of affairs arising within a very few years. In the second place, the deterioration in certain areas took place so rapidly in the first part of the nineteenth century that any information secured from informants alive since 1900 is completely useless. Unless very good documentary evidence is available for such areas, there is no recourse but to fall back on the method of extrapolation and area comparisons.

The principal Spanish accounts upon which we must rely include a few which have been published. Most of them, however, are to be found in manuscript form in the Bancroft Library, University of California, Berkeley. Some of them were translated for an unpublished manuscript by the Late Professor Herbert I. Priestley and several were translated for Dr. C. H. Merriam. Merriam's translations are on file in his manuscript collection. The citations to these accounts, published and unpublished, are given in the manuscript section of the Bibliography. In this text they are referred to, without further citation, by the author's name and date.

## THE TULARE LAKE BASIN

We may commence detailed consideration of the aboriginal population with the Tulare Lake Basin, which was inhabited in 1800 by three Yokuts tribes, the Wowol, Tachi, and Chunut (see maps 1 and 2, area 2). The first official visitor to the area was Father Juan Martin who entered the valley in 1804 in search of new mission sites. He found the principal village of the Wowol, which he called Bubal. This rancheria, he said, contained not less than 200 children. It was visited again in 1806 by Moraga, who found 400 inhabitants. Eight years later Father Cabot passed the site and found 700 people. Subsequently, it was visited by Ortega in 1815 and Estudillo in 1819 but these writers gave no population figures. Since no other village was ever recorded by name in the territory of the tribe, it is safe to assume that there was no other, at least of permanence and reasonably large size.

Gifford and Schenck (1926), in their discussion of the history of the southern valley, conclude that because the village was reported as having 400 persons in 1806 and 700 in 1814 there was a real increase in population during the intervening eight years. This they ascribe to fugitives from the coastal missions who entered the valley as refugees. The opinion expressed by these authors may serve as the starting point for discussion of certain general problems which are encountered in attempting to estimate the aboriginal population of the valley.

In 1804 Martin saw 200 children. If we knew the ratio of children to adults, we could easily compute the total number of inhabitants. The age of "children" was variously estimated in colonial New Spain, indeed all the way from seven to fifteen years. The early California missionaries used approximately fourteen years for males and twelve for females. In 1793, however, the system was standardized for doctrinal purposes. Indians, both gentile and converted, were designated as children if they were under ten years, i.e., in the age bracket from 0 to 9 inclusive. Hence all the clergy conformed to the method in so far as they were able and unless they specified otherwise.

There are certain data available which permit us to estimate rather closely what proportion of the population in California should be regarded as falling within the category of children. Within the missions the annual censuses enable us to compute with accuracy that the individuals under the age of ten years, between the dates 1782 and 1832 averaged 21.4 per cent of the total population (Cook, 1940). This value is relatively high and may not conform to gentile, or aboriginal, conditions. With regard to these we have information from archaeological sources. In the Museum of Anthropology at Berkeley there are several hundred skeletons excavated from habitation sites in central and northern California, the ages of which have been determined and which constitute a fair cross section of the native population during the centuries immediately preceding invasion by the white man. Of these skeletons 22.6 per cent represent persons dying under the age of twenty years, and perhaps 10 or 15 per cent persons dying under the age of ten.

Further light is shed by the baptism records of the missions San Jose and Santa Clara (these are discussed in greater detail in a later paragraph) which list gentile baptisms according to village and distinguish between men, women, and children. In the two missions, from approximately 1805 to 1833 there were baptized a total of 5,217 persons from villages in the valley region. Of these 930, or 17.8 per cent were children and 1,939, or 37.1 per cent were listed as men. The sex ratio is 0.826. Evidently the natives captured and brought to the missions do not give us a completely true picture of the composition of the aboriginal population, despite the large sample at our disposal. It is highly probable that (1) the natural sex ratio was nearly unity and (2) many of the men were killed in warfare or escaped the clutches of the convert hunters. Therefore we are justified in setting the number of men equal to that of the women. If we do this, the population represented by the 5,217 conversions was actually 5,626, of which men and women each constituted 41.8 per cent and children 16.4 per cent.

Finally, we have figures from Zalvidea (MS, 1806) with respect to villages at the extreme southern end of the San Joaquin Valley. (These are discussed subsequently in connection with the population of that area.) At two of these, after adjusting for disturbed sex ratio, he found respectively 13.5 and

9.6 per cent children. However, Zalvidea's account states specifically that in these villages he carries the age of childhood only through the seventh year. If he had counted as children those under ten years of age, the percentages would naturally have been higher.

The data just set forth render it abundantly clear that the children constituted between 10 and 20 per cent of the aboriginal population. Since the exact value can never be ascertained, it is wholly reasonable to establish the arbitrary figure of 15 per cent. If we apply this factor to Bubal the result is not less than an aggregate of 1,333 persons, much greater than the value set by Moraga in 1806.

With respect to the suggestion of Gifford and Schenck that the number of inhabitants of Bubal had been augmented between 1806 and 1814 by refugees from the missions the following points may be noted. In the first place, it has been possible to show (Cook, 1940) by means of the mission censuses that in 1815 the cumulative total of fugitives reported by all the missions in the colony amounted to 1,927 persons. Of these a great many who ran away in the earlier years were deceased. Many never went to the valley at all and the remainder were distributed from Sacramento to Bakersfield. It is highly unlikely that as many as 300 would be concentrated at one village such as Bubal. In the second place, the majority of the fugitives who did reach the village or its vicinity were former inhabitants of the locality who were merely returning to their old homes rather than coastal Indians, who would have constituted real refugees. On the whole, therefore, and this conclusion applies throughout the valley, true increase of population by immigration of foreign fugitives was negligible.

A further problem of importance illustrated by our data for Bubal is the extent to which population estimates for villages were affected by local fugitivism or temporary scattering of the natives at the advent of the Spaniards. Very frequently the explorers left notations that the inhabitants of a certain rancheria had fled, or that many were absent. It seems clear that even by the year 1800 the natives were all too well aware of the purpose of the missionaries and soldiers and took measures to defeat that purpose. For this reason, remarkable as it may appear, the largest estimates are likely to have been the most accurate.

Returning now to the population of Bubal we find Martin counting "no less" than 200 children in 1804, indicating a total number somewhere in the vicinity of 1,300, although most of the adults apparently had absconded. In 1806 the same situation arose and Moraga found only 400 left in the village. In 1814 Cabot estimated that the village contained 700 people, despite the fact that some may have been missing. The apparent increase in 1814 can be very simply explained by the assumption that fewer natives had fled the village than had done so when Moraga arrived. Cabot's figure may be quite near the truth for the year 1814 since we must concede a drastic overall reduction of population in the area between 1804 and 1814. Certainly the population can never have been less than 700. The weight of the evidence at hand thus indicates that the estimate based upon Martin's account, i.e., 1,300 persons, is essentially sound.

Further evidence of collateral importance is derived from consideration of the location of the village of Bubal. Gifford and Schenck (1926, p. 27) place Bubal on Atwell's Island, near Alpaugh, in T23S, R23E, that is, on the east side of Lake Tulare. Neither Martin (in 1804) nor Moraga (Muñoz diary of 1806) locates the rancheria with any precision but Cabot (1815) left San Miguel on October 2, 1814, and on October 3 traveled over an immense plain, arriving late in the day at Bubal, on the shore of a big lake. This can have been only Lake Tulare and the west shore thereof. The next year Ortega (1815), approaching from the north or northwest, passed through Sumtache (i.e., Chunut) and went on to Bubal, where he arrived late at night, not having been able to find the village "... por haverse mudado de su sitio propio ..." Estudillo was the next visitor who has left us a detailed account of this area. On October 22, 1819, he went from near Cholam to a place called Los Alisos near the edge of the foothills of the coast range. On October 23 he went across the plain and on October 24 arrived at Bubal, obviously from the west, and found it deserted, adding the comment that the village "... manifesto aver ya dias q. se fueron a otra parte." The following day he pushed five leagues south through tule swamp and found the settlement on the bank of the lake although his soldiers had to wade waist deep for two leagues farther in order to catch most of the inhabitants. Apropos of this incident he says regarding Bubal: "Esta es la rancheria de gentiles mas immediata a las misiones, y la q. con mayor frecuencia se hacen cristianos en la de San Miguel."

From these accounts it is very clear that the original site of Bubal was on the west, not the east, shore of the lake and that because of the depredations of the Spaniards the inhabitants fled into the lake itself, where they made at least temporary settlements. That these became their permanent home is attested by the fact that no later than 1826 Pico stated that Bubal was situated on an island in the lake. Subsequently contemporary writers as well as the modern ethnographers agree that the principal village of the Wowol was on Atwell's Island.

From the demographic point of view the chief justification for tracing the migration of Bubal in the first two decades of the nineteenth century is to indicate how the constant pressure of the Spaniards, through incessant military expeditions, could affect the population. Through a series of years, their native village site having become untenable, the people of Bubal were forced to seek precarious and inadequate shelter where-ever they might find it in the depths of the tule swamps until ultimately they could establish themselves in a new home, an island fortress where they might remain relatively undisturbed. Starvation, casual massacre, and disease coupled with exposure must have strongly reduced the total number. Hence a 50 per cent decrease in ten or fifteen years—from Martin to Cabot and Estudillo—is not at all surprising.

The Chunut were first visited by Martin in 1804, who designated their principal rancheria Chuntache but gave no population figures. Two years later, in 1806, it was seen by Moraga, who called it Tunctache and said it had 250 people. Cabot in 1814 said there were 700 persons and Ortega in 1815 found 20 males. Estudillo in 1819 found 103 young braves ("indios gallardos mozos") and 200 women, old men, and children. However, he also states that the captain and "la mayor parte de la gente" were away on a visit toward Lake Buenavista.

The estimates of Cabot and Estudillo appear to be quite reliable. Cabot describes Bubal and then passes on to Suntache. The latter place he says had a population "about the same as the preceding," or 700 persons. Since Estudillo took the pains to count the young men precisely, his remaining estimate must be fairly correct. The total thus is 303 persons present plus more than the same number of absentees, or approximately 700.

Since the location and history of Tuntache was very similar to that of Bubal and since in the period 1815-1819 the population was nearly the same, it is very probable that there was a reduction in population at the former village analogous to that seen at the latter. Although we have no concrete data, such as Martin's report for Bubal in 1804, which may be applied to Tuntache, it may be assumed with safety that the aboriginal inhabitants of this rancheria numbered at least 1,200.

The third lake tribe was the Tachi. This tribe, or its principal village, was first recorded by Martin in 1804. He gives no direct figures but implies that there were 4,000 inhabitants, although he may have been referring to the entire lake area. The next visitor of consequence was Cabot in 1814 who stated that Tache "... segun presenta y por la caseria que la compone ..." had 1,000 souls. At a distance of two leagues he found another rancheria, Guchame, which may have belonged to the same tribe, which "... segun presenta y informes tomados no pasara de 200 almas ..." The next year Ortega attacked the rancheria but the people had been warned and had all fled when he entered. They had not returned, moreover, in 1819, when they were seen by Estudillo. They must have been in bad straits, because Estudillo found them living deep in the swamp, in a "gran Bolson de Tule, sin poder tener lumbre." Estudillo gives no figures but he makes the interesting comment that the Tachi had four chiefs and that the rancheria (or tribe) had several "parts," each at some distance from the others. This raises the question whether Cabot saw the only rancheria of the tribe or one of a number. The village he saw he examined sufficiently carefully to enable him to count the houses. Such an arrangement is incompatible with rancherias "each at some distance from the others." Furthermore four chiefs would imply four more or less equal subdivisions, or four rancherias and possibly 4,000 inhabitants. At first sight this appears preposterous. However, the following facts should be noted.

1. The area held by the tribe extended across the north and west shores of Lake Tulare from the present town of Lemoore to Coalinga close to the western foothills. This comprises a greater area than the Wowol and Chunut together.

2. Modern informants have been able to give the ethnographers Kroeber, Gayton, and Latta the names of 3 villages for the Wowol, 2 for the Chunut, and 8 for the Tachi. Although the number of villages has no strict quantitative significance, it does indicate the greater size of the Tachi.

3. As mentioned previously, Derby in 1850 found the Tachi tribe to contain about 8000 individuals, of whom 300 lived in the principal rancheria. In view of the very great attrition to which all the open valley tribes had been subjected between Estudillo's visit in 1819 and that of Derby in 1850 it is almost incredible that the Tachi should have diminished only from 1,000 to 800 during that period. It is much more reasonable that the principal village should have declined from 1,000 to 300 as would be indicated by the figures of Cabot and Derby. If so, then the tribe as a whole must have once contained much more than 1,000 people.

4. Father Martin in the description of his trip implies that there were 4,000 people living in the vicinity of Tache. It has generally been assumed, and is so stated by Gifford and Schenck (1926, p. 22), that Martin was referring not only to the borders of Lake Tulare but also to the lower reaches of the Kaweah and Kings rivers. This is simply an assumption and rests upon no unequivocal evidence.

5. Cabot's quite careful estimate for the principal rancheria
shows that it was larger than Bubal or Tuntache in 1814.
Martin's data for Bubal showed that this town must have
contained fully 1,330 persons in 1804. If we disregard any
shrinkage prior to that year, the contemporary population of
Tache would have reached at least 1,600 if Cabot's estimates
for the two villages in 1814 are to be credited.

On the basis of all these facts the author believes that the Tachi aboriginally possessed one village with at least 1,600 inhabitants and that Cabot's figure for this village was reasonably accurate. In addition, the statements of Estudillo in 1819 and Derby in 1850—and both of these observers were trustworthy persons—point definitely to the existence of at least three other villages. These were undoubtedly smaller than the principal rancheria. In default of any concrete data each may be estimated as half the size of Tache, or 800 persons apiece. The total for the tribe would then be 4,000 or nearly twice as much as for the Wowol and Chunut combined.

An aggregate of 6,500 natives for precontact times seems to be indicated in the Tulare Lake basin. The figure 1,100 was obtained for the period of approximately 1850-1852. The reduction would then have been to a value of 16.9 per cent of the aboriginal level. If this seems excessive, it should be borne in mind that the area was subjected to the ravages of disease, both epidemic and venereal, from 1770 forward, as is attested or implied by both Garcés in 1776 and Martin in 1804. It was overrun by clerical and military expeditions in 1804, 1812, 1814, 1815, and 1819, not to mention an indefinite number of private raiding parties which have left no trace in the documents. From 1820 to 1850 it was entered repeatedly by ranchers from the coast, American trappers of the Jedediah Smith variety from the southwest or north, and by New Mexican bandits. All these took a toll in the form of mission converts, battle casualties, burnt food stores, and disrupted village life. Finally, it should be remembered that the dry and arid plains of modern Kings, Tulare, and Kern counties bear no resemblance to the former region of rivers, sloughs, swamps, and lakes which once supported uncounted millions of game birds and animals, together with a luxurious vegetation capable of supporting a very dense human population.

<u>TULARE LAKE BASIN ... 6,500</u>

## THE KAWEAH RIVER

Together with the Tulare Lake Basin the lower Kaweah River and its delta from Lemon Cove to below the town of Tulare was probably one of the most densely populated spots in California, or possibly even north of the Valley of Mexico (see maps 1 and 3, area 3). The repeated comment of the missionaries with respect to the "infinidad de gentiles" to be found there creates a subjective impression which is borne out by the numerical data we possess.

There seem to have been two rather indistinctly separated divisions of the region. One, centering around Visalia and occupying the delta and sloughs, contained three tribes, the Telamni, Wolasi, and Choinok, of which the Telamni were the most important and numerous. The other, centering around Lemon Cove and probably extending some distance into the lower foothills, included the Wukchamni, Gawia, and Yokod, the largest group being the Wukchamni.

Martin entered the delta in 1804 and called the people Telame. Moraga in 1806 explored it more thoroughly. According to the Muñoz diary (Oct. 19-20), the party noted Telame with 600 souls, together with a "big rancheria" one league east and the rancheria Cohochs two and one-half leagues east. In addition there were "otras varias rancherias" in the vicinity. The village list appended to the diary gives Telami I ("tendra segun corto computo 600 almas"), Telame II with 200 souls, Uholasi with 100, Eaguea with 300, and Cohochs with 100. Uholasi is no doubt Wolasi, and Eaguea and Cohochs are probably respectively Gawia and Yokod. If the last two are omitted, it is evident that Moraga saw or knew about four rancherias, Telame I and II, Uholasi, and the unnamed big rancheria. To these must be added the "otras varias rancherias," which may have amounted to another four, or eight in all. A population of 2,000 to 4,000 is certainly indicated.

Cabot in 1814 was the next visitor who left a record. He referred to the "Roblar de Telame Rio," which included Telame, the largest rancheria in the Tulares. Cabot's Telame may well have included both the villages to which this name was ascribed by Morgan. If so, on Moraga's figures it must have contained a minimum of 800 persons. A higher number is more probable, however, in view of the fact that it was the largest in the area.

In 1816 Father Luís Antonio Martinez passed through the region and left a circumstantial account of his visit. Starting from Bubal, he approached the Telame area, reaching first the village of Gelecto, where "... encontraron no mas el cementerio: se habia destruido por las guerras ..." These wars apparently were raids and skirmishes in which refugees from the missions and other Indian villages participated. From Gelecto the party went to Telamni "... al llegar alli los divisaron de Lihuauhilame el grande ... done al dia anterior habian tenido una gran refriega cuyo resultado fue dar muerte a únos 8 hombres ..." The captain of the latter rancheria sent a messenger to Martinez with the report the place contained "como de 300 casados."

Gelecto was one league from Lihuauhilame and since the latter village could be seen from Telame the distance between the two could not have been more than a league. Martinez then went six leagues south to Quihuama, before proceeding westward on the way home.

Lihuauhilame contained 300 married men, or heads of families. The aboriginal social family consisted of at least five persons, and even after the disruption suffered from 1804 to 1816 must have amounted to four. The total population, according to this assumption, must have reached fully 1,200, with a probable pre-invasion value of at least 1,500. Martinez therefore gives us four sizable places: Gelecto (depopulated), Telame (minimum 800 according to Moraga and Cabot), Lihuauhilame (1,200), and Quihuama.

Subsequent visitors (e.g., Estudillo, 1819, and Rodriguez, 1828) mention Telame but give no data with respect to size nor do they specify any other rancherias in the immediate vicinity. For basic population data we are consequently forced to depend upon Cabot, Moraga, and Martinez.

In the discussion of Bubal mention was made of the attrition of population due to war and disease during the period following the first entry of the Spaniards in or about the year 1800. That these factors were very serious becomes even more evident from the accounts of the Telame region. Martinez describes the total obliteration of Gelecto, which he ascribes to the "wars." Elsewhere in his report he refers to much internecine fighting among villages and between natives and fugitives from the missions. Moreover, the Spanish accounts repeat ad nauseam the statement that this or that village was attacked or destroyed in the course of various expeditions, or that village after village was deserted by its inhabitants because of fear of the soldiers. It is highly probable that there is a great deal of lost history pertaining to the central valley during this period and that tremendous destruction was inflicted upon the native villages which was never recorded in the official documents.

Hunger and disease were likewise rampant. Clear indication of this condition is contained in the sentence of Ortega, in 1815, with respect to Telame: "... encontrando esta grande rancheria toda desparramada por la mucha mortandad que havian tenido, y la much hambre que padecian ..." With regard to the cause of the "mortality" it is clear that a part was due to the killing by the Spaniards and other Indians during the "wars," a part was due to famine, and very likely the remainder was due to disease. Although this factor is not specifically mentioned, the word "mortandad" was widely employed by the Spaniards and Mexicans to connote the effects of an epidemic. Furthermore, the absence of disease would be more difficult to explain than its presence in view of the wide intercourse between the peoples of the southern valley and those of the coast at a time when the Indians of the missions were dying by thousands from measles, dysentery, and other contagious maladies introduced by the whites. The whole picture is one of ruinous devastation in the Kaweah delta just prior to 1816, with accompanying disorganization of the local economy and reduction of population.

The effect of war, disease, and starvation cannot be emphasized too strongly, nor can mention be made of them too often. On account of their debilitating influence the populations seen in the Kaweah delta and reported in the documents cannot possibly be overestimates of the aboriginal number. On the contrary, they undoubtedly represent too low, rather than too high, a figure.

Reverting now to the villages reported, Moraga mentions eight places, four of them by name or other specific reference. Martinez mentions four, all by name. Cabot refers to Telame as the largest village in the Tulares. Elsewhere (MS, 1818) he states that before reaching Telame there are five rancherias, including Quiuamine and Yulumne. Quiuamine is no doubt the Quihuama of Martinez.

Telame was one village, according to all observers except Moraga (actually Muñoz, who wrote the diary). Moraga ascribes 600 people to the first Telame and 200 to the second. The first estimate, be it noted, was "segun corto computo," or according to a short count. The estimate must therefore on Moraga's own admission be increased, certainly to 1,000 and perhaps more. In view of the size of the well known rancheria Bubal, fully 1,300, Telame must have contained 1,200 persons.

In addition to the two Telames Moraga mentions a "big rancheria" one league to the east. Hence there were three villages which comprised what may be termed the Telame complex. No figures were given by Moraga for the unnamed rancheria, since it was entirely deserted. However, since it was regarded as "big," there must have been several hundred inhabitants, say 500. The total for the triad then would have reached nearly 2,000.

The Martinez description is apparently somewhat at variance with that of his predecessor. Martinez saw, cites distances for, and mentions by name three rancherias: Telame, Lihuauhilame, and Gelecto. They were located within a radius of one league of each other and must correspond to the three seen by Moraga. Gelecto was in ruins, with only the cemetery still in evidence. Hence Gelecto may very well have been the big, deserted rancheria of Moraga. Martinez gives no population data for Telame but says there were 300 heads of families in Lihuauhilame, which was, therefore, without much doubt the largest of the three. According to Moraga's figures,

Telame I was the largest. Hence the concordance seems to be that Telame, Lihuauhilame, and Gelecto of Martinez correspond respectively to Telame II, Telame I and the "big" rancheria of Moraga. As pointed out previously, the total inhabitants to be deduced from 300 heads of families, under the conditions existing in 1816 was 1,200. This is twice the estimate of Moraga.

An important point arises here with respect to Moraga's estimates. At Bubal, it will be remembered, Martin found evidence of 1,300 people in 1804 whereas Moraga reported only 400 in 1806. At Lihuauhilame Martinez found according to the statement of the village chief 1,200, although Moraga had reported ten years previously only 600. Furthermore Cabot, at Bubal eight years after Moraga, found 700 persons. For these two important villages therefore Moraga differs flatly with three other competent authorities by a factor of two or three. Similar instances may be found elsewhere in which Moraga's population figures are far too low. It seems difficult to escape the conclusion, consequently, that Moraga (or Muñoz) consistently underestimated the native population. The reason is not immediately apparent, although several possible suggestions may be offered. Moraga personally had little interest in such matters. Although he himself did not write the account of the expedition to the Tulares in 1806, he did write that of his expedition to the Sacramento Valley in 1808. The latter diary shows very clearly, through the extreme paucity of its population data, that Moraga either made no direct counts or estimates, or considered them too unimportant to mention in his manuscript. For the 1806 trip the estimates were all supplied, obviously, by Muñoz. There is no reason to impugn either the judgment or veracity of this missionary. However, if one examines his account, it becomes evident that Muñoz based his figures either (1) on statements of gentiles or (2) on the number of natives seen by him. The former source might or might not be accurate. The latter was almost certain to yield too low values because the Moraga expedition was notoriously hostile to the natives and at nearly every village approached the inhabitants fled if they could possibly do so. Muñoz therefore consistently saw only the residue, a fraction of the actual number.

For the above reasons the writer believes that a correction factor should be applied to the Moraga-Muñoz data, and unless there is specific reason to believe otherwise, the figures should be regarded as indicating only about 50 per cent of the true population. Such a correction should not be applied to the figures of other explorers, like Cabot or Estudillo, who were far more careful in their methods of estimate.

If, now, we apply a correction factor of 2, Moraga's estimate for Telame I becomes 1,200, or the same as that found by Martinez for the same village (Lihuauhilame). On the same basis Telame II (Telame of Martinez) would have had 400 persons. Gelecto (unnamed by Moraga) was "big" but probably not as big as Telame I. Hence we may assume an intermediate value, say 800. The total for the Telame complex, or the triad of villages, would have been 2,400.

In addition to the triad we have Uholasi and the "otras varias rancherias" of Moraga. Since Moraga gives 100 for Uholasi we may increase that number to 200. Among the other rancherias we have Quihuame (or Quiuamine) and Yulumne, which were noted by later visitors. Moraga, however, in saying "otras varias" clearly means more than two, probably at least four. It is pertinent to note in this connection that some of these may have disappeared during the turmoil of 1806 to 1816 and that their surviving inhabitants may have been absorbed by other, larger villages. Such an explanation would account for the failure of Cabot and Martinez to refer to them. If we assume four villages at the time of Moraga's expedition (and of course the aboriginal number would have been no less), it is safe to consider them as having been relatively small. According to the size scale of the Kaweah villages as a whole 200 inhabitants could reasonably be ascribed to each of them, or 800 for the group.

The aboriginal population of the Telamni and the Wolasi may therefore be set as closely as we can get at 3,200. The Choinok appear to have had only one rancheria. At least there is one and one only which recurs repeatedly in the Spanish documents. This is Choynoque (Moraga, 1806), Choynoct (Ortega, 1816), Choinoc (Cabot, 1818) or Choijnocko (Estudillo, 1819). Moraga gave 300 as the population, as did also Estudillo. The two values are comparable, if we remember the attrition occurring between the years 1806 and 1816. We may then apply the correction factor of 2 and get 600 as the most probable number in 1806. Such a value is also consistent with the status of the Choinok as an independent tribal entity of the Kaweah basin, although it does not take into account any reduction in population prior to the expedition of Moraga. There was doubtless such a reduction, but since we have no direct evidence bearing upon the matter it will be better to let the figure 600 stand.

The total for the Kaweah delta group (Telamni, Wolasi, Choinok) is 3,800. This is indeed surprising but the figure perhaps is corroborated by the statement of the Franciscan President for the California missions, Father Payeras—made in support of the establishment of new missions in the valley—that the Telame district alone contained 4,000 unconverted heathen.

The middle Kaweah above Visalia was inhabited by the Gawia, Yokod, and Wukchamni. The Gawia are represented in Moraga's account by Eaguea (300 inhabitants) and the Yokod by Cohochs (100 inhabitants). The

Wukchamni were by far the most numerous and for an excellent account of them we are indebted to Estudillo. This officer, in addition to being a competent field commander, appears to have been a scholar and a gentleman. His report on the Wukchamni village of Chischa is unquestionably the most complete and accurate left us by any of the Spanish explorers and as such is worth discussing in detail.

Estudillo was the first white man to see Chischa. On this point he is very explicit:

> ... su capitan joasps, ni su gente jamas havian visto tropa,
> siendo esta la primera vez q. havilan llegado alli, pues hace
> mucho tiempo paso por abajo (este fue D. Gabriel Moraga en
> el reconocimiento q. hizo en 1806) y solo noticia tubo por sus
> amigos de Telame ...

Consequently, allowing for possible communicable disease, Chischa was in its aboriginal state when Estudillo saw it.

Chischa was 5 leagues east of Telame and 3 leagues from Choinocko. This places the village, according to the maps of Kroeber and of Gayton, at or just above Lemon Cove in the territory ascribed by these ethnographers to the Wukchamni. Estudillo measured off the dimensions of the village by pacing. The shape was semilunar, crescentic or approximately that of the sector of a circle. The short side ("por su frente") was 624 varas long and the long side ("por la espalda") was 756 varas. A figure plotted on coördinate paper to scale shows that the area was 80,000 square varas. On the assumption that the Spanish vara equaled a yard, and that an average city block measures 300 feet on a side, the village of Chischa would have covered eight city blocks.

Estudillo caused the Indians living in the village to form a line before the town, with the men in a single file and the women and children massed in front of them. He counted the men and found that there were exactly 437 warriors ("jovenes de arma") and "como 600 mugeres y ninos." According to the translation made for Merriam (MS in his collection):

> Then I went opposite where the invited guests were lodged,
> and as they all, men and women and boys and girls were
> presented to me in a confused mass, I could not count them
> as I did those of Chischa but there were perhaps 600 men."

He specifies the 600 men as "jovenes" and adds that there were 200 "mugeres jovenes." He then describes going behind the village to the arroyo, where he saw more than 100 "mugeres de mayor edad," washing seeds for atoles for the celebrants of the fiesta, and an even greater number of "jovenes moliendo en piedras dhas semillas."

The extraordinary care with which Estudillo conducted his investigation can leave little doubt of the accuracy of his figures. He saw 437 "jovenes de arma" in front of the village together with 600 women and children, plus 100 "mugeres de mayor edad" and more than 100 "jovenes" behind the village preparing the meal. Even allowing for some duplication of individuals the population must have reached at least 1,250. The solidity of this evidence for Chischa renders even more probable comparable figures for Bubal and the other large villages of the general area.

Estudillo saw 600 young men and 200 young women who were visitors. If we use the same ratio of young men ("jovenes de arma") to total population for these groups as for Chischa, then the 600 young men represented a total of 1,700 persons. These were all, says Estudillo, from the "roblar," or the Kaweah basin. When he arrived at the village, he was met by seven chiefs (who were already on the scene), two from Telame, one from Choynoco, and four from other rancherias of the "roblar" near the sierra. We may assume that the seven visiting chiefs were accompanied by approximately equal retinues, or 114 persons each. If two of the chiefs and 228 persons came from the Telame district and one chief with 114 persons from Choynoco (i.e., Choinok), then the remainder, 458, were from other tribes. By the same proportionality factor these represented a total of 980, or let us say 1,000, Indians. The Wukchamni and their satellites must therefore have numbered 2,250 individuals in the year 1819. Estudillo himself says that the population of Chischa and its neighbors was 2,400, but he may have included some Telamni among this number. On the other hand, the visitors to Chischa on the occasion of the fiesta could scarcely have included all the inhabitants of the villages whence they came. Some, for one reason or another, must have remained at home. Hence the estimate of 1,000 is probably under the true value.

Now it is important that Estudillo was in the "roblar" in 1819. In view of the severe disorganization, "mortality," and "famine" of 1814 to 1816, the population of the Wukchamni must have undergone a serious decline before Estudillo saw the tribe. Despite the absence of any specific figures the documents give the impression that the reduction of population around Tulare Lake was almost complete by 1819 and that the valley tribes along the margin of the foothills had lost fully half their number. It will be proper therefore to ascribe a one-quarter reduction to the Wuchamni, Gawia, and Yokod. If we accept Estudillo's estimate of 2,400 for the year 1819, the aboriginal population for these groups would have been 3,200.

In the meantime the Mono of the upper river had scarcely been touched, save possibly by epidemics of which we have no record. It is significant that at the great gathering at Chischa there appeared, near the middle of the day, a chief with 69 men and 42 women from a rancheria called Apalame in the interior of the Sierra Nevada. These natives, probably Balwisha or Waksache, had never seen troops. To arrive at the population of the entire Kaweah basin in aboriginal or proto-aboriginal times these tribes must be included. Their strength, as previously estimated, was of the order of 600 persons.

Computing now the total for the Kaweah river and delta as first described by white men, we find an aggregate of 7,600 inhabitants. As set forth previously, the survivors in 1850 numbered about 1,800 or 23.7 per cent of the aboriginal (or early historical) value. Excluding the relatively undisturbed Mono the comparable value for the lower river and delta is 17.2 per cent. These percentages are in close agreement with those found for the ecologically similar area bordering Lake Tulare.

KAWEAH RIVER ... 7,600

## THE MERCED RIVER

It will be convenient at the present juncture to consider the watershed of the Merced River, although this area lies at a considerable distance from that just examined (see maps 1 and 4, area 6).

In the preceding section it was concluded that only 500 to 600 natives still remained in 1850 on the lower portion of the river below the foothills, whereas the population of the southern Miwok in the foothills and higher ranges amounted to approximately 1,250. The latter figure was based principally on Merriam's village lists and the population counts obtained from informants by Gifford for the Miwok farther north. The question must now be propounded whether these data, which appear to be fairly accurate for the year 1850 or even 1840, can be taken as showing the population under substantially aboriginal conditions, let us say those obtaining prior to the intense Spanish invasion of the valley in the decade 1800 to 1810.

1. As a matter of generalization it can be stated that the environment as remembered by the oldest informant or even his parents can scarcely reach into pre-Spanish times. Hence the village populations and distributions as reported in good faith to Gifford or Merriam must have been subjected in some measure to the disruptive effect of the white man. The great disturbance in the valley itself, which was manifested by the entire extinction of whole Yokuts and Plains Miwok tribes, must have had repercussions in the near-by hills through disease, kidnaping, and minor dislocation of food supply,

even though the actual territory of the natives was not physically invaded by the newcomers. Hence, a priori, one might anticipate that the populations as derived from ethnographic sources would be somewhat less than truly aboriginal.

2. In the discussion of Gifford's data on the North Fork Mono it was shown, on the basis of persons per family and houses per village, that the population in the memory time of the informants was about 440 whereas the precontact value must have been nearer 640. The population residue in 1840-1850 would then have been 68.8 per cent of the aboriginal level.

3. For the upper Tuolumne and Stanislaus Gifford's population figures were based upon the values given by his informants for 49 villages. The average was 20.8 persons per village, a number which was accepted as valid for the period of 1850. The distribution of population for the villages is as follows:

| Inhabitants per Village | Number of Villages | Number of Persons |
|---|---|---|
| 60 | 1 | 60 |
| 55 | 1 | 55 |
| 35 | 3 | 105 |
| 30 | 6 | 180 |
| 25 | 8 | 200 |
| 20 | 9 | 180 |
| 15 | 6 | 90 |
| 10 | 12 | 120 |
| 5 | 1 | 5 |
| 0 | 2 | 0 |
| Total | 49 | 995 |

Now it may be assumed that under normal conditions few if any villages would contain less than 20 persons and that those listed by Gifford with 15 or less were the victims of a general decline in numbers. Hence to the latter may be ascribed a minimum of 20 persons. At the same time the other villages must have suffered some reduction. Although there is no positive evidence bearing on the matter, it would not be excessive to add five persons to each of the others. Making these corrections the total becomes 1,340 instead of 995. The residue in 1850 would then be 74.2 per cent of the aboriginal level. Incidentally, the inhabitants per village would then be only 27.35, a value by no means excessive for prehistoric times.

Some confirmation for these assumptions can be obtained by further consideration of Gifford's study of the North Fork Mono. As previously mentioned, Gifford shows the number of houses and hence the number of families living in the hamlets of this tribe. For many hamlets two or more sets of houses are given, implying consecutive, not simultaneous, occupancy. The average number of houses per hamlet occupied at one time is 2.7. However, informants were able to recollect an additional 44 houses, which had been formerly used. Including these, the average number per occupied hamlet is 3.21. Gifford's family number is 4.89, a value which may be increased to 6.0 to cover aboriginal conditions. Thus the mean size of an active prehistoric Mono hamlet may be taken as 19.25, or let us say 20 persons. Since the Mono villages were intermittently inhabited whereas those of the Miwok were permanent and probably somewhat larger, the average value of 27.35 for the latter seems in no way excessive.

From the above considerations the conclusion is warranted that for the northern Mono and the Miwok the population as derived from good modern ethnographic data is about 70 per cent of the precontact value. The estimate for the upper Merced, derived from Merriam's village lists was 1,239. If the factor of 70 per cent is applied, the aboriginal population becomes 1,770.

For the lower Merced Valley we are dependent entirely upon the account of Moraga's visit in 1806. Coming from the west, he crossed the San Joaquin River on September 27 and moved three leagues north to camp on or near Bear Creek in T8S, R10E. The following day, September 28, Moraga divided his expedition and sent one group north and another northeast to explore. Both groups found a great river, with many natives, all of whom fled on seeing the white men. At least one rancheria was found, because Moraga "adquirio la noticia de otras 5 rancherias sitas en el rio fuera de aquella en que se hallaba del parte de 250 almas, segun el informe de los gentiles." On the 29th the camp was moved three leagues ENE (more probably NNE) to the river, the Merced. There were two rancherias on the river bank, the people of which had fled through fear of the white men. On the 30th a party went up the Merced and found many natives "sin duda de sus 5 rancherias."

Moraga then went north and returned to the Merced on October 7. The Spaniards saw many natives and were visited by 79 warriors from the rancheria "del otro lado del rio," i.e., on the south bank. The 8th of October the expedition visited the rancheria just mentioned; to judge by the number of men (the women having fled) the rancheria had 200 souls. This place was called Latelate, and there was another village near by, called Lachuo, with the same number of inhabitants. The next day the expedition moved on southeast.

Moraga evidently saw two villages and heard of about five others. The two which he saw, Latelate and Lachuo, are said, on the basis of the warriors seen, to have contained 200 persons each. Since warriors of one village, Latelate, numbered 79, the estimate of 200 total inhabitants, or a ratio of 2.5 to 1, is entirely reasonable. If the other five villages had the same number, the aggregate for the river would have been 1,400. However, some of the others may have been larger. In the list of rancherias appended by Muñoz, the approximate sequence of the journey is followed. Five rancherias can be ascribed logically to the Merced: Chineguis, Yunate, Chamuasi, Latelate, and Lachuo. Chineguis follows Nupchenche in the list, Nupchenche having 250 souls and Chineguis the same population. Likewise, Yunate and Chamuasi have the same "segun compute regular." Latelate and Lachuo are given 200 each, thus corresponding to the text of the diary. The other two villages are not mentioned by name in the list but it may be presumed that they were of approximately the same size, let us say one of 250 souls and the other of 200. Thus the Muñoz-Moraga count gives us 1,600 inhabitants.

It will be remembered that the figures cited by Moraga for the population of villages in the Kaweah-Tulare region were uniformly at variance with those of other observers and were always too low. Hence a question may be raised with respect to his data for the Merced valley. The villages in this area, by all subsequent accounts, were smaller than in the heavily populated territory farther south. Furthermore, Moraga's was the first expedition of which we have record which explored the Merced Basin. These facts would tend to indicate that Moraga's figures may be reasonably accurate. On the other hand, the repeated statements that the Indians fled on the approach of the white men and the fact that estimates had to be made from the number of warriors seen leave the possibility open that there actually were more people than Moraga thought. Hence it will be reasonable to ascribe an aboriginal population of 250 to each of the seven rancherias, giving as a total 1,750 for the lower Merced River.

The population of the entire valley then would have been 3,520, or, rounding off to the nearest hundred, 3,500. The survivors along the lower river amounted to approximately 550 in the year 1852. If the population in Moraga's time was 1,750, then the reduction from 1806 to 1852 was to 31.4 per cent of the original level. In view of the somewhat more remote position of the Merced, this figure checks quite well with the values found on the Kaweah River and Lake Tulare.

MERCED RIVER ... 3,500

# THE KINGS RIVER

The next region to be considered is the basin of the Kings River. Like the Kaweah, this stream may be divided into three sectors. The first comprises the delta and slough area southwest of Kingsburg and was the home of the Yokuts tribes, Apiachi, Wimilchi, and Nutunutu (area 4A). The second includes the valley margin and foothills, with the tribes Wechihit, Aiticha, Choinimni, Chukamina, Michahai, and Emtimbich (area 4B). The third is in the higher foothills and embraces the territory of the Mono groups, Wobunuch and Holkoma (area 4C).

The Kings River sloughs were first described in 1804 by Martin, who mentions the tribe, or rancheria, of Notonto (Nutunutu) but gives no population data. The next visitor was Moraga in 1806. In the diary of the expedition, written by Father Muñoz, no mention is made of Notonto but in the appended "List of rancherias visited in this trip and the one in April" are included Notonto I with 300 persons and Notonto II with 100. Estudillo saw the region in 1819 and said that Notonto (only one village of this name is mentioned) had 303 men "todos gente robusta y de armas." He also saw a few old women and children. Since the men are of the same type ("robust warriors") and were carefully counted in the same way as at Chischa, the same ratio of warriors to total inhabitants may be used. A population of 866 is thus indicated or, in round numbers, 850. Estudillo also says there were four chiefs, one each of the "Notontos," Gumilche, Guchetema, and Tateguy. The Nutunutu are thus clearly segregated from the Wimilchi (Gumilche). The other two names cannot be traced and may indeed have been those of individuals. The "guimilchis," in the meantime, had been seen in 1815 by Pico, who says that they had at least two rancherias.

From the ethnographers we get indication of six villages: of the Apiachi, the village of Wohui (Kroeber, Gayton, Latta); of the Nutunutu, the villages of Chiau (Kroeber, Gayton, Latta), Hibekia (Kroeber), Honotau (Gayton), and Kadestiu (Latta); of the Wimilchi, the village of Ugona (Kroeber, Gayton, Latta). If these villages actually existed in the early years of the nineteenth century, they can scarcely have held less than 250 persons apiece and the population would have been in the vicinity of 1,500.

From the Spanish accounts we find evidence of at least four villages: originally two (perhaps later one) of the Nutunutu and two of the Wimilchi. One of the latter may have been in fact the principal village of the Apiachi. The Nutunutu, whether as a single village or as a tribe, seem to have amounted to fully 850 persons at the time of Estudillo. Since these groups had been exposed to expeditions beginning in 1804, it is very probable that they had undergone considerable attrition before they were observed by Estudillo.

This point of view is supported by Estudillo's remark that he requested the warriors of Notonto to meet him without their weapons because this rancheria "es la mas velicosa y terrible de los Tulares." Hence it is quite probable that the aboriginal population reached 1,200. A value of 500 may be assigned arbitrarily to the other villages or tribes, for Estudillo mentions three chiefs apart from the Notontos and Pico says that the Wimilchi had at least two rancherias. The probable aboriginal population for the entire area is therefore 1,700.

By the year 1850 the tribes of the Kings River delta were represented, according to the account of G. H. Derby, only by the rancheria of Notonto which then had 300 inhabitants. The population had thus fallen to 17.6 per cent of its former value. A footnote to the decline of the native inhabitants in this region is the fact that within a year or two after Derby's visit the village of Notonto was attacked by American cattlemen and farmers. The rancheria was devastated and 200 of the 300 people present were massacred in cold blood.

For the second sector of the Kings River we are dependent primarily upon the record of the Moraga expedition. Moraga and Muñoz evidently covered the river from the vicinity of Reedley to, or nearly to, the junction of the main stream and Mill Creek. The villages mentioned by them belonged principally to the Aiticha and the Choinimni. The Wechihit and the Toihicha may have been included but the Chukamina, Michahai, and Emtimbich seem to have been overlooked. Hence the figures given by Moraga are undoubtedly incomplete.

On October 16, 1806, having arrived from the San Joaquin River two days previously, Moraga sent out two scouting parties. One went upstream and found a rancheria of "como de 60 almas," called Ayquiche (or Aycayche). They were no doubt among the Aiticha, above Sanger. Here they heard about, but did not see, six other rancherias "sitas a la orillas del rio por la parte de la sierra." The other party went downstream and found three villages close together on a spacious plain along the banks of the river. They had a total of 400 inhabitants, but most of the people had fled. The "List of rancherias visited in this trip and the one in April" gives the names of these villages: Aycayche, which "according to the Indians" had 200 people, Ecsaa with 100, Chiaja with 100, and Xayuase with 100. In addition there was Capitau, which was very small and a "sugeto" of Xayuase. It had about 10 people. Apparently in October Muñoz and Moraga found only 60 Indians left in Aycayche, whereas in April they learned that it really contained 200. The difference must be ascribed to fugitivism.

The three downstream villages are credited by the "List" with 100 inhabitants apiece, but the diary states that there was a total of 400. The latter figure is more likely to be correct. Thus, with Aycayche, Moraga saw in this sector four villages and 600 persons. The other group of villages, six in number, was farther toward the mountains and no particular information concerning them is given in the diary. The "List," however, is more explicit. Under Aycayche it is stated:

> Aqui hay otras 6 rancherias que no se pudieron reconocer
> y son todos, segun la noticia de los indios de esta rancheria
> como del porte de almas de Pizcache.

Pizcache is said to contain 200 souls. An aggregate of 1,200 persons is therefore indicated or, for the entire region seen by Moraga, 1,800.

The middle course of the Kings River has been discussed in the preceding section and it has been pointed out that in the middle of the nineteenth century this region was relatively heavily populated. The accounts of several contemporary observers indicate that in 1850 or thereabouts somewhere between 2,000 and 4,000 natives were still to be found between the remnants of the Nutunutu on the west and the foothills Mono on the east. The ethnographic data supplied by Kroeber, Gayton, Latta, and Stewart show approximately 25 villages remembered by informants. If we use the fairly conservative average of 150 persons per village, the total is 3,750. To assume 3,500 is merely to stay within the bounds of the existing evidence.

If we accept tentatively 3,500 as the number of Indians on the middle Kings River in midcentury, then we are confronted with the problem of backward extrapolation. For the Tulare-Kaweah region the probable decline from 1800 to 1850 was probably to the level of approximately 20 per cent of the original value. Direct application of this factor to the Kings River gives a value for 1800 of 17,500. This is manifestly far too high. For the Mono and the Miwok in the upper foothills many facts point to a population decline to approximately 70 per cent of the prehistoric value. Application of this factor gives 5,000 for the Kings River, a high but not impossible figure.

Other considerations are worth mention at this point. In his diary of 1826 José Dolores Pico describes his adventures on the Kings River in January of that year. He was chasing stock thieves and trying to recover stolen animals. From January 10 to January 14 he beat back and forth along the Kings River, from the sloughs to the foothills, attacking every Indian in sight. The results were discouraging. He captured no animals, killed not over a score of natives, and was completely outmanoeuvered by the combined forces of the Wimilchi, the Notontos, and Chukamina. The entire tenor of the document suggests an active, competent, and quite powerful local confederacy of tribes. This diary of Pico describes the only expedition to the Kings River of which we have documentary knowledge between 1806 and the coming of the Americans.

These facts suggest, first, that there was a sizable population which managed to maintain itself reasonably well for several decades along the Kings River. Secondly, they suggest that there may perhaps have been a slow migration of the more exposed valley people, like the Nutunutu, higher up the river. Both these factors would tend to keep the population decline to a minimum.

In view of the confusion surrounding the evidence in this area and in view of the apparent inadequacy of the Moraga figures the aboriginal population of the middle Kings River may be set at 5,000, with the full realization that this value represents the best guess under the circumstances.

The upper river was inhabited by the Mono groups, Holkoma and Wobonuch, for which an 1850 population of 1,700 was computed. The decline to 70 per cent may be accepted here without serious reservation; hence the original number would have been 2,340. Adding the values for the three sectors of the river we get 9,130 or, estimating to the nearest hundred, 9,100.

KINGS RIVER ... 9,100

## UPPER SAN JOAQUIN, FRESNO, AND CHOWCHILLA RIVERS AND MARIPOSA CREEK

The area between the Merced and the Kings rivers (see maps 1 and 4, area 5), which includes the courses of the upper San Joaquin, the Fresno, and the Chowchilla rivers, together with Mariposa Creek, is very poorly represented in the early documentary sources. The central valley itself, as far as the foothills, was apparently traversed by numerous expeditions and raids, and the population was largely missionized, killed, or dispersed. The written record is, however, quite inadequate. It is therefore not feasible to consider each of these river systems separately, as was done in the discussion of the population about 1850. It is preferable to discuss the entire region as a unit and, when necessary, pass to indirect methods of estimate.

The Pitkachi on the San Joaquin are mentioned in 1806 by Moraga, who allows 200 persons to their rancheria. The tribe appears again in the baptism record of Soledad Mission (MS in the Bancroft Library, Berkeley) according to which 205 Indians from "Picatche" were baptized from 1821 to 1824 and another 18 in 1831. An additional 23 came from rancherias in the vicinity, a total of 246. Another rancheria, Capicha, is referred to by Pico in 1815, who said it was uninhabited at that time, the inhabitants having fled to the mountains. As late as 1853 Wessels said that the Pitcache, together with the Noo-to-ah, a Mono group, numbered 500 to 600 souls. Kroeber mentions three villages remembered by modern informants.

If 246 Indians were baptized in one mission, the tribe as a whole must have numbered at least four times as many, or 1,000. If two fair-sized rancherias are mentioned by the Spanish observers, the entire tribe may well have possessed four or five, which again implies a population of 1,000. If there were approximately 300 survivors in 1853, by comparison with other open valley areas the original population must have been fully three or four times as great, or perhaps 1,200. If three rancherias were known to modern informants, they must formerly have been important places with anywhere from 200 to 400 people, again indicating a total of 1,000 for the tribe.

Concerning the Hoyima there are two references, one by Pico in 1826 and one by Rodriguez in 1828. Pico states merely that he attacked the rancheria and captured 40 gentiles and 1 Christian, a fact which in itself would not furnish a very significant clue to population. He also noted "mucha guesamenta y cueros casi frescos de caballada que habian matado."

The account by Rodriguez is more circumstantial. This soldier went along the San Joaquin River in late April of 1828. On the 24th he sent a group of men to scout the "rancheria de los Joyimas, que es adonde an comido la caballada." At dawn the next day they attacked the village, "que estaba en medio de los dos brazos del rio" (the San Joaquin west or northwest of Fresno). He captured 26 Indians and 27 animals (horses). Another 60 or 80 horses escaped "en el monte." At about this time a gentile captain came from a rancheria designated Guche or Getche, depending upon how one deciphers the handwriting of the manuscript. He "vino a los Joyimas a comer caballo." The rancheria named here is probably that of the Heuchi on the Fresno River. This gentile said there was another rancheria "mas arriba" at which there were horses. Rodriguez sent Simeon Castro to investigate. He found no one at the rancheria mentioned but went on 2 leagues to another rancheria, likewise deserted but containing the carcasses of 100 dead horses, which had been slaughtered and were about to be eaten. It was noted by Rodriguez that: "Estas 3 rancherias son una misma que es la de los Jaimes." It was also remarked that the rancheria was divided when the horses arrived in order to eat with less fear of detection. From this account it is clear that the Joyimas had at least three villages. Allowing somewhat over 300 persons each, the population of the group would reach 1,000.

The slaughtered horses open up an interesting field of speculation. It is clear that by 1828 large segments of the aboriginal population had entirely given up the sedentary ancestral mode of life in favor of an existence based upon stock raiding. To do this it was necessary to recast village life completely—as is suggested by the fact that the rancheria was "divided" when the horses arrived. In order to catch the horses for food other horses were essential for rapid transportation to and from the coastal settlements. New arts and skills had to be learned, and new categories of labor had to be evolved.

Rodriguez found among the Hoyima as a whole 87 to 107 live horses (27 captured, 60-80 in the wilderness), which were presumably about to be killed and eaten, together with 100 animals already slaughtered. The total thus reached approximately 200. The question now is pertinent: how much food can be obtained from 200 horses? If we assume that each of these relatively light range animals weighed 800 pounds, we may deduct about 25 per cent to account for bones, hide, certain of the viscera, and other inedible parts, leaving 600 pounds which the Indians could and did consume. The aggregate is 120,000 pounds of meat. If this meat was dried and preserved, according to general practice, it was sufficient to supply 329 persons the equivalent of one pound of fresh meat per day for one calendar year. If it had to be consumed immediately or within a few days, and if every man, woman, and child ate 20 pounds apiece, it was adequate for 6,000 people. If the entire tribe, not merely one rancheria, divided the meat into equal shares, and if the tribe numbered 1,000 persons, then the share of each individual amounted to 120 pounds. Whether these figures are strictly accurate is irrelevant. They merely emphasize that a quite sizable group must have been concerned. We may therefore regard the Hoyima as being as large a tribe as the Pitcache, and estimate that the population was at least 1,000.

The remaining two tribes in the valley proper, as listed by Kroeber and others, were the Heuchi and the Chauchila. They occupied the north bank of the Fresno River and the distributaries of the Chowchilla River. The ethnographic data include no more than one or two villages for each tribe. The Heuchi are referred to by Rodriguez, who says that the rancheria of the "Jeuche" was completely deserted. However, since it was the principal tribal village, it must have contained at least 200 persons. The Chauchila were also noticed by Rodriguez, who says that at "Chausila" he "captured" 142 people and "killed many." If we concede that as many escaped as were captured or killed, there must have been fully 400 in all.

The Nupchenches, although they are merely mentioned as a possible tribe by Kroeber (Handbook, p. 485) and are doubtfully recorded by Schenck (1926), occupied an important position in the early nineteenth century. Indeed, the failure of Kroeber and Schenck to consider them seriously makes it necessary to set forth in some detail the information about them contained in the Spanish reports.

These natives were distributed along the San Joaquin River from its big bend near Mendota to approximately the mouth of the Merced (see map 4, area 5A). The first mention of them is by Moraga in the diary of 1806. He found two rancherias, Nupchenche with 250 people and Cutucho with 400 souls which was "junto a la primera llamada Nupchenche." This means that Cutucho was close to but at that time not necessarily part of Nupchenche. From the description in the diary Nupchenche was situated at or near the mouth of Santa Rita Slough in T9S, R12E, and this is almost exactly where Schenck places it on his map (Schenck, 1926, p. 133). The next visitor who left a record was José Dolores Pico in 1815. On November 7 he left San Luis Gonzaga in western Merced County (in approximately T10S, R8E) and went east to the Tulares at "Arroyo nombrado San Jose," which was close to the rancheria of the Cheneches. At dawn of the 8th he attacked the village and captured 66 persons, but "... la mayor parte de esta gente se fue pr estar dha rancheria en mal parage." The gentiles said that 4 leagues up the San Joaquin River was Nupchenche, thus placing Cheneches on the river in the southern part of T8 S, R11E. This location checks well with the statement made elsewhere in the diary by Pico that Cheneches was near the junction of the San Joaquin and "Las Mariposas," or Mariposa Creek. If Pico captured 66 persons but "the majority" escaped, the total number must have reached from 200 to 400, if not more.

Pico then scouted Nupchenche and learned that all the inhabitants had fled. He therefore by-passed the village and went 8 leagues southeast up the San Joaquin to the rancheria Copicha. This rancheria, which by the way must not be confused with the Cutucho of Moraga, was thus located on the river several miles north of Firebaugh, probably near or in T11S, R13E. As a check on this location is Pico's further statement that Copicha was in the valley of the San Joaquin "junto del Tecolote," or the Chowchilla. On November 10 he moved 8 leagues southeast from Copicha and saw horses from the rancheria Tape, which, from the distances, was near Mendota. This view is supported by Estudillo, who saw the region in 1819 and says that the spot "... donde Tape tenia su rancheria" was 24 leagues south of Cheneches and 25 leagues north of Notonto. Actually, Mendota appears to be approximately halfway between these two points.

Pico mentions one other village, Malim, which he places near Cheneches. Confirmation is found in a letter of Fr. Marcelino Marquinez (MS) on May 25, 1816, stating that the Cheneches recently have killed two Christians from Malim. The latter rancheria thereupon allied itself with Notoalh and Luchamme. No other trace of the two last-named villages is found.

Other writers who mention the Nupchenches group include Fr. Antonio Jaime, who mentions Cutuchu (MS, 1816) as a rancheria from which Soto brought back gentiles, and Ortega, who, in his 1815 diary, mentions Cupicha as having been attacked by Pico. Finally Inocente Garcia in his manuscript of 1878 records an expedition against the Nupuchineches under Ignacio Vallejo. The rancheria, even in the 1830's was "muy Populosa." The expedition captured 100 warriors and 300 of all ages and sexes, arguing a population of over the 300 claimed as captives.

From these accounts emerge six rancherias, each of which is mentioned independently by at least two writers. From north to south they were: Cheneches and Malim, Nupchenches and Cutucho, Copicha, Tape. Moraga says Nupchenches had 250 people and Cutucho had 400. From Pico's statement concerning captives we may ascribe a minimum of 300 to Cheneches, and Copicha, Malim, and Tape can scarcely have been much smaller. Hence the entire group can have numbered no less than 1,800 in 1816.

At Tape on November 23 Pico found 16 live horses and mules recently killed together with "mucha carne enterciada." If we neglect the meat, 254 whole animals, dead or alive, were actually counted. From November 25 to 28 the party traveled steadily from Tape to Cheneches. From Tape to Cheneches inclusive they saw 500 dead horses. It is not clear whether the 238 animals seen at Tape were included in this figure. If, however, assuming that they were, we use the same ratio of dead horses to inhabitants as was discussed with respect to the Hoyima, these villages should have contained 2,500 persons. This figure is quite reasonable if we grant that the horses were to be consumed by the entire group of villages, rather than only one or two of them, and may be provisionally accepted.

On the basis of the records presented, a probable population value for the valley floor between the Merced and the Kings rivers in the decade 1810-1820 was 5,100. But this may well be an underestimate and be representative of the aboriginal population. Evidence pointing in this direction is the almost complete obliteration of these tribes before 1850. That very serious attrition was going on among these exposed people is evident from the records of all the explorers. The massacre and kidnaping described by Pico is itself significant. In addition, we have the discussion by Estudillo in 1819, who found almost the entire surviving population of Tape sick and dying. He also points out that at the moment there were no less than four expeditions, including his own, ranging up and down the open valley, bent upon destruction. To explore the problem further indirect methods must be employed. We may therefore turn to estimates based upon stream distances.

If minor local variation is disregarded, the habitat provided by the Merced and the Kings rivers from the lower foothills out to the center of the valley is in no essential respect different from that characterizing the Mariposa, the Chowchilla, the Fresno, and the San Joaquin throughout its length below the foothills. The native villages were spaced more or less uniformly along the larger rivers. Hence an approximate proportionality should have existed between riverbank distance and the number of inhabitants. No high degree of precision can be expected from calculations based upon these premises but the method yielded rational results for the period centering around 1850 and from it the correct order of magnitude should be obtainable.

Airline distances are used for the rivers. The general course of all the streams is substantially straight and the numerous small meanders are uniform in size and occurrence throughout the area. Three river sectors are used as a basis: the lower Merced River, the middle Kings River from and including Mill Creek to Kingsburg plus the principal tributaries, and the lower Kings from Kingsburg to Lemoore. The data are compiled briefly as follows in tabular form.

| River Sector | Miles in Length | Population | Persons per River Mile |
|---|---|---|---|
| Lower Merced | 32 | 1,750 | 55 |
| Middle Kings | 75 | 5,000 | 67 |
| Lower Kings | 20 | 1,500 | 75 |

Despite the uneven nature of the basic information these figures show considerable internal consistency. The mileage of the San Joaquin, Fresno, Chowchilla, and Mariposa amounts collectively to approximately 190 miles (the four streams west of Kroeber's line of the valley Yokuts and down the San Joaquin as far as the mouth of Bear Creek). At 65 persons per mile (the approximate mean of the three values cited above) the population would be 12,350, or, let us say an even 12,000. This is more than double the number indicated directly by the Spanish accounts. It has been pointed out, however, that these accounts are incomplete with respect to the villages seen and recorded. Furthermore the records demonstrate a condition of severe disorganization on the part of the native society. Hence the indirectly computed figure may reflect more closely the aboriginal population level.

The population in 1850 for the part of the Yokuts territory here being discussed was considered in a previous section. The best estimates were found to be 1,000 for the Mariposa and Chowchilla and 2,900 for the Fresno and San Joaquin. The total, 3,900 is 32.5 per cent of the estimated aboriginal population and represents, therefore, a reduction of the same general extent as was demonstrated for the Kaweah-Tulare Lake region.

The foothill region drained by the four rivers being discussed includes the extreme northern Yokuts tribes, the North Fork Mono, and some of the southern Miwok. In the consideration of the 1852 population it was not advantageous to segregate river sectors as has been done for the earlier data. This is because, with certain exceptions, the data pertaining to the later period cover as a rule the entire stretch of each river, rather than the central valley plain as distinct from the foothills. Nevertheless it is possible to arrive at the result desired indirectly.

For the Yokuts on the middle Fresno River it was concluded that the average number of inhabitants per village was 60. This value was based on village numbers and general estimates for the period of 1850 and included also the assumption that the villages had been much reduced in size by that year. For precontact times it is quite justifiable to maintain that the average size was of the order of that demonstrated for the Kings and the Merced, or let us say 150. The tribes on the Fresno and San Joaquin not seen or at least not reported by the Spanish writers are the Gashowu, Wakichi, Kechayi, Dumna, Toltichi, Dalinchi, and Chukchansi. The total number of villages recognized for these seven tribes by Kroeber, Gayton, and Latta is 36. This total of course rests on the memory of informants and pertains to conditions in the period 1840 to 1850 or perhaps 1860. There is no proof whatever that the village number in 1800 was the same, yet the whole history of Indian-white contact in the valley region leads one to believe that it can hardly have been smaller. Since there is no evidence to the contrary and since the hypothesis is inherently reasonable, we may concede 36 villages of 150 persons each or 5,400 in all.

For the southern Miwok on the upper Mariposa and Chowchilla, calculated by means of village counts and Gifford's average of 21 Indians per village, the values of 273 and 410 respectively were obtained. The factor of a reduction to 70 per cent of the aboriginal population may be here applied, yielding a total of 975 for the two streams. The figure for the North Fork Mono in prehistoric times has already been placed at 640.

If we now add 12,000 for the valley and marginal Yokuts, 5,400 for the foothill Yokuts between the Miwok border and the Kings River, 975 for the southern Miwok on the Mariposa and Chowchilla and 640 for the North Fork Mono the total becomes 19,015.

The validity of this figure can be subjected to a check through comparison by area. This method cannot be expected to show up minor or secondary errors but it will bring to light any fundamental or serious discrepancies.

We may block out four major regions: the Kaweah-Tulare Lake, the Kings River, the Merced River, and the segment between the Merced and the Kings. Each of these represents fundamentally the same type of environment, i.e., a rough strip extending southwest to northeast, beginning with the lakes and sloughs of the central valley axis, passing across the valley floor to the foothills, and reaching ultimately the middle altitudes of the Sierra Nevada. Four cross sections are thus obtained, differing in width but fairly uniformly including the habitats represented. It should be noted that the water surface of Lake Tulare as it existed in 1860 has been deducted from the area of the Kaweah-Tulare region; also that the two northern regions include a relatively greater expanse of uninhabitable mountain territory than do the two southern regions. The western boundary has been drawn along a line approximately five miles west of the San Joaquin River and the prolongation of its axis toward the lake. The westward extension of the Tachi toward Coalinga had to be neglected since there are no clear tribal boundaries in this area. The number of square miles was computed by township lines and the error of estimate must be considered at least plus or minus 20 per cent. The results follow:

| Region | Area (sq. mi.) | Population | Population density per sq. mi. |
|---|---|---|---|
| Kaweah-Tulare | 1,880 | 14,100 | 7.12 |
| Kings | 1,530 | 9,100 | 5.85 |
| Merced | 1,400 | 3,500 | 2.50 |
| Mariposa-San Joaquin | 3,760 | 19,000 | 5.05 |

The density of the Mariposa-San Joaquin area is quite close to that of the Kings River Basin. The Kaweah-Tulare territory has a somewhat higher density, but this finding is compatible with the known enormous concentration of population around Tulare Lake and in the Kaweah delta. The value for the Merced strip is unduly low. The discrepancy can be accounted for on two grounds. The first, already mentioned, is that this river, throughout its length, passes through a greater area of uninhabitable mountains than do many of the other streams. The second is that our estimates for the lower Merced are insufficient. They rest in essence on the single report by Moraga, who, as has been shown, tended to underestimate and who did not see, or at least did not report upon, the entire course of the lower river. Moreover there is no report at all from Spanish sources with respect to the San Joaquin between the mouth of the Chowchilla (Nupchenche group) and the mouth of the Tuolumne. That villages did exist throughout this region is attested by the illuminating account of J. J. Warner, who was a member of Ewing Young's expedition to the great valley in 1832 and 1833. (I use the text as quoted in Warner, 1890.) He says (p. 28):

> In the fall of 1832 there were a number of Indian villages on King's River, between its mouth and the mountains: also on the San Joaquin River from the base of the mountains down to and some distance below the great slough. On the Merced River from the mountains to its junction with the San Joaquin there were no Indian villages; but from about this point on the San Joaquin, as well as on all of its principal tributaries, the Indian villages were numerous; and many of these villages contained from fifty to 100 dwellings.

It is noteworthy that Warner saw no villages on the lower Merced, precisely at the spot where Moraga in 1806 had recorded no less than seven. All of these must have been obliterated during the intervening twenty-six years, striking testimony to the devastation being wrought among the open valley peoples. But from the junction of the Merced and the San Joaquin rivers, along the main axis of the valley the villages were numerous, some of them containing 50 to 100 houses or at least 250 to 500 people.

What happened to these villages is graphically told in Warner's own words.

> On our return, late in the summer of 1833, we found the valleys depopulated. From the head of the Sacramento to the great bend and slough of the San Joaquin, we did not see more than six or eight Indians; while large numbers of their skulls and dead bodies were to be seen under almost every shade-tree near water, where the uninhabited and deserted villages had been converted into graveyards; and on the San Joaquin River, in the immediate neighborhood of the larger class of villages, which, in the preceding year, were the abodes of a large number of those Indians, we found not only graves, but the vestiges of a funeral pyre. At the mouth of King's river we encountered the first and only village of the stricken race that we had seen after entering the great valley.

This was the pandemic of 1833, concerning which, in comparison with some accounts, Warner's description is a model of conservatism.

It is evident that a combination of circumstances prevents us from making an adequate assessment of the aboriginal population of the lower

Merced River and adjacent segments of the San Joaquin. Our density figure is about half the expected value. If we had the full facts, we could perhaps double the estimated population. Under existing conditions we can feel reasonably sure of the value given for the area between the Mariposa and the San Joaquin rivers.

MARIPOSA-SAN JOAQUIN ... 19,000

## THE SOUTHERN SAN JOAQUIN VALLEY

The southern end of the valley, beyond Tulare Lake and the Kaweah River, can best be considered in three parts. The first is the foothill strip from the Kaweah to the Tejon Pass, which was inhabited by the Yokuts tribes Koyeti, Yaudanchi, Bokninuwad, Kumachisi, Paleuyami, and Yauelmani (maps 1 and 2, area 1G). The second comprises the lower Kern River together with the former Buenavista Lake basin. This area was held by the Yokuts tribes Hometowoli, Tuhohi, and Tulamni. The third includes the peripheral fringe of relatively high foothill and mountain country of the southern Sierra Nevada and Tehachapi and was inhabited by non-Yokuts people: Tubatulabal, Kawaiisu, Kitanemuk, and the Tokya branch of the Chumash (maps 1 and 2, areas 1A to 1E).

Only the Koyeti are described by the Spanish authorities hitherto consulted. Moraga mentions the rancheria Coyahete with a population of 400 in 1806. Estudillo in 1819 found a rancheria, which he called Arroyo de Copaipich, with 200 and one called Canyon Agspa with 400 people. The latter may perhaps be Moraga's Coyahete. If so, the tribe had a population of at least 600 in 1819, but it must have suffered some decline prior to that year. Latta's informants were able to remember 8 villages. Moreover, the tribe was oriented ecologically toward the Kaweah delta and oak forest, although it was actually situated on the lower Tule River. Thus an estimate of 800 persons would not be too much for the precontact period. The Yaudanchi on the upper Tule River also, according to Kroeber and to Latta, had 8 villages and covered considerably more territory than the Koyeti. Hence the same population may be ascribed to them. The Bokninuwad were evidently a smaller group, since Kroeber reports for them only two villages and Latta none. It would not be safe to allow them more than 200 persons. If we do so, then the tentative estimate for the three tribes must be put at a total of 1,800.

For the remainder of the territory held by the Yokuts there are only two documentary references, the diaries of Garcés in 1776 and Zalvidea in 1806. Both these writers give population data which have been subject to considerable controversy.

For the Buenavista region the four pertinent villages are mentioned by Zalvidea and are as follows:

| Village and Tribe | Houses | Men | Women | Children | Total |
|---|---|---|---|---|---|
| Malapoa (Tulamni) | ... | 29 | 22 | 8 | 59 |
| Buenavista (Tulamni) | ... | 36 | 144 | 38 | 218 |
| Sisipistu (Hometwoli) | 28 | 50-60 | ... | ... | ... |
| Yaguelame (Yauelmani) | ... | 92 | ... | ... | 300 |

From even casual inspection it is apparent that Zalvidea did not see the complete population of any one of these villages and that many of the inhabitants had been removed by previous expeditions or were in hiding. The village of Malapoa is small but presents no serious demographic discrepancies. The number of children was low, but as has been pointed out in a previous discussion Zalvidea was counting as men or women everyone over the age of seven years. The children, calculated according to his method, amounted to 13.5 per cent of the total.

At Buenavista he found only 36 men to 144 women, an incredible situation unless most of the men had fled or had been killed. Under normal conditions the number of men should at least approximately equal that of the women. Therefore in order to reconstruct the probable population we are forced to assume the presence of at least 144 men. This gives a total of 326 persons of which 8.6 per cent would have been children. For the other two villages only the number of men is given, no doubt the men actually seen. Indeed at Yaguelmane Zalvidea "counted" the 92 men he specifies. Significantly, however, he counted men "from 7 to 40 years" and infers that the village had a population of 300. If for Yaguelmane we allow 10 per cent of children seven years old or younger the adults would number 270. If the sex ratio were near unity, then, with 92 men 40 years or younger, there must have been 47 men over that age and 135 women of all ages. If the same ratios are applied to Sisipistu with 55 men from 7 to 40 years of age, the population would be 180. This figure is quite consistent with the number of houses, 28, for the number of persons per house would then be 6.43. The four villages (Malapoa, Buenavista, Yaguelame, and Sisipistu) consequently must have had populations of 59, 326, 300, and 180 respectively. The average of the four is 191 persons.

Since there are no other historical data pertaining to the lake region, it is necessary to utilize the village lists of Kroeber (1925) and Latta (1949). These investigators, through their informants, have located 3 villages for the Hometowoli, 1 for the Tuhohi, 3 for the Tulamni, and 2 for the Yauelmani of the lower Kern River, making 9 in all. As suggested with respect to other areas the number of villages was undoubtedly as great in 1806 as in 1840 or 1850. Hence we can be assured of at least 9 in 1806. For size it is proper to use Zalvidea's average of 191 inhabitants, thus giving as the population of the Buenavista basin 1,720.

For the southern foothills we must rely upon the diary of Garcés. Gifford and Schenck (1926) discuss this document at length, concluding (p. 21) that the population actually seen by Garcés north of the slopes of the Tehachapi was 750 and that the total population "south of the Tule River" was 1,000 to 1,500. Since the present writer must differ from these authors, it is worth while to review once more the evidence furnished by the Garcés account. In so doing the exact route of the explorer must be made plain.

On May 1, 1776, having previously descended the southern mountains to the valley floor, Garcés broke camp:

> Having gone one league northwest I came upon a large river
> which made much noise, at the outlet (al salir) of the Sierra
> de San Marcos and whose waters ... flowed on a course from
> the east through a straitened channel.

(Coues, ed., 1900, pp. 280-281). The river of course was the Kern and the spot was without question the point at which the river suddenly breaks out onto the plain from its canyon. The water was here swift ("made much noise"). It literally "sallied forth" from the mountains, and its course from the east was through a narrow channel. This place is about 14 miles east-northeast of Bakersfield on California State Highway 178.

Garcés then went downstream "a little way" and found a rancheria (no. 1) on the right bank. After going a little way farther he saw a rancheria (no. 2) on the left bank and another (no. 3) "to the west." He went downstream no more than 2 or 3 miles, otherwise, as was his invariable custom, he would have specified his distances in leagues. Three rancherias can therefore be located on the Kern between the last abrupt slope of the eastward hills and just below the mouth of Cottonwood Creek. These correspond on the map to Kroeber's villages Altau and Shoko of the Paleuyami and Konoilkin of the Yauelmani, although the actual identity is by no means assured.

After crossing the river with difficulty Garcés struck northwest "and a little north" for 3 leagues. This brought him to a stream where there was a rancheria (no. 4). From a point 3 or 4 miles below the entrance of the Kern River canyon a line running northwest by north extends diagonally about 7 miles across T28S, R29E to reach Poso Creek near the northern boundary of the township.

After passing the night at the rancheria mentioned (no. 4), Garcés went straight north for 4½ leagues. On the way he went by some deserted rancherias. These villages were not temporarily deserted, with the inhabitants in hiding. They were "rancherias despobladas," that is, permanently depopulated or abandoned. It is interesting to speculate on the cause of this phenomenon, for the depopulation can have been due only to intertribal warfare or disease. We know nothing of any native wars of sufficient magnitude to have destroyed several whole villages. On the other hand, as Garcés himself later points out, Spaniards had already penetrated the region. Pedro Fages was in the southern valley in 1772 on his way to the Colorado and Garcés found at least one deserting soldier living with the Indians. It is quite possible that decline of population had already begun as early as 1776.

After traveling 4½ leagues Garcés found another rancheria (no. 5), at which he spent the night of May 2-3. This must have been somewhere near the hamlet of Woody at the southern boundary of T25S, R29E. On May 3 he moved another 2½ leagues, still north, to reach the White River near or slightly to the west of the village of White River in T24S, R29E. Here he camped at a rancheria (no. 6) of 150 souls. On May 4, having reached his farthest point north, he visited another rancheria (no. 7) half a league east. At rancheria no. 6 he found an Indian who was a fugitive from the coast and also heard that two Spanish soldiers had been killed for molesting Indian women. The contact with the whites was therefore clearly established. Stephen Powers (1877), who was in the San Joaquin Valley in the decade of 1850 says that "on White River there are no Indians, neither have there been any for many years." Here again is an indication of depopulation at a very early date.

On May 5 Garcés started to retrace his steps southward, reaching at 2½ leagues the previous rancheria (i.e., no. 5). From here he must have diverged somewhat eastward of his northbound trail for at 2 leagues he saw another rancheria (no. 8) "to the east" which he had not seen on the way up. This probably was toward the eastern side of T26S, R20E. Then, he says, he went southeast 3 leagues to Poso Creek. This would put him on Poso Creek near the center of township T27S, R30E, a point about 9 miles airline above his place of crossing on May 2. Here he found a rancheria (no. 9), the chief of which told him about another rancheria (no. 10) to the east where a Spanish renegade lived with an Indian wife. The following day, May 6, he started out again south or southwest and got lost in the hills of upper Poso Creek. In these hills between Poso Creek and the Kern River he found another rancheria (no. 11) of "more than 100 souls." This was probably in the northern part of township T28S, R30E. Finally on May 7 he reached the Kern 1 league above his first crossing. His first crossing had been accomplished 2 or 3 miles below the mouth of the canyon hence he must have come out very close to the mouth. He then went downstream to the rancheria where he had crossed (no. 1) but he did not stop here. He continued down the river for 2 leagues to a rancheria he had not seen before (no. 12) and which had "some 150 souls."

Two leagues downstream from rancheria no. 1, or about 3 leagues below the mouth of the canyon would have put him at a point roughly 5 to 6 miles east-northeast of Bakersfield, not at the site of the city, as is supposed by Coues (1900, p. 299). On May 8 he went 3 leagues south-southwest, then turned and traveled 6 leagues southeast and east to the Tehachapi. These distances and directions plotted on the map place him just at the mouth of Tejon Creek.

To summarize the rancherias mentioned: Garcés saw four villages on the Kern in territory of the Paleuyami or Yauelmani (nos. 1, 2, 3, 12), six on Poso Creek or minor watercourses to the north thereof (nos. 4, 5, 8, 9, 10, 11), all Paleuyami, and two on White River (nos. 6, 7) in the territory of the Kumachisi.

The size of these villages has been subject to some debate. Garcés cites two with 150 persons and one with 100, but Gifford and Schenck think that he specifies population only for the largest places. The other nine would therefore be smaller. These authors, however, put the average village size at about 60 (750 people in 12 villages). Deducting 400 for the three rancherias specified, the average of the other nine would be 39 which seems much too low. If Zalvidea's figures are any criterion, the villages on the Kern should have averaged at least 100 inhabitants, and it must be noted that Garcés found two rancherias in the hills with 150 and 100 persons respectively. Thus it seems reasonable to allow an average of 100 rather than 60. If so, the population seen by Garcés was in the vicinity of 1,200.

Now it is evident that Garcés did not see all the villages in the region. He covered about 10 or 12 miles of the Kern below the canyon, a good deal of upper Poso Creek, and perhaps 5 miles of White River. He never reached the lower stretches of the rivers at all. It is fair to assume that there were as many rancherias which he did not see as there were seen by him. If so the estimate of the population should be doubled, making 2,400.

One secondary piece of evidence is at hand. Garcés saw 8 villages of the Paleuyami (6 in the hills, perhaps 2 on the Kern). Now Zalvidea in 1806 says that the Pelones (Paleuyami) had at that time 13 rancherias. Allowing for shrinkage in the intervening thirty years, this is twice the number seen by Garcés.

We may at this juncture have recourse to river mileage estimates. It was found previously (p. 36) that for the Stanislaus, Tuolumne, Merced, Mariposa, and Chowchilla there was in 1850 0.34 village per mile of stream, with the Chowchilla having the lowest value, 0.20 village. For the Merced and the Kings rivers below the foothills in the first years of the nineteenth century it was calculated that there were on the average 65 persons per river mile. Assuming that the average village size was 150 inhabitants, there would have been 0.44 village per river mile. The southern streams were probably more sparsely inhabited than those just mentioned. Hence it is reasonable to apply the factor found for the Chowchilla, 0.20 village per mile, to the White River, Poso Creek, and the Kern River. There are about 150 miles of stream in these systems east of a line running from Porterville to Bakersfield, a line which Kroeber takes as the approximate westward limit of the foothill tribes. This means a probable 30 villages. If the average of 100 persons per village is used, as suggested above, this means a population of 3,000. The direct documentary approach thus gives 2,400 and the indirect method 3,000. A fair figure would be the mean of the two, or 2,700.

The peripheral hills on the southeast and south were held by several tribes. The entire upper Kern River, above the present village of Bodfish, belonged to the Shoshonean group, the Tubatulabal (area 1E). Kroeber thinks they may have reached a population of 1,000, which seems a reasonable figure. From the Kern and Walker's Pass south to Sycamore Creek (area 1D) were the Kawaiisu, a tribe, according to Kroeber, of 500 persons. In the southeastern corner from Sycamore Creek to Poso Creek were a few Yauelmani and the Kitanemuk. Pastoria Creek and Alisos Creek were occupied by a northward extension of the Alliklik, and from Alisos Creek westward to Bitter Water Creek were found the Tokya group of the Chumash.

For the groups beyond the Kawaiisu there are no population data of any kind. Even Kroeber fails to make an estimate. If we say 1,000 for them all in aboriginal times it will be a pure guess, but one which may be somewhere near the truth in view of the extent and character of the terrain involved. The total for the peripheral region would then be approximately 2,500 and that for the southern end of the valley as a whole 6,920, or in round numbers 6,900.

SOUTHERN SAN JOAQUIN VALLEY ... 6,900

# THE NORTHERN SAN JOAQUIN VALLEY

The remaining portion of the Yokuts-Miwok territory lay in the valley and foothills north of the Merced River. This area (see maps 1 and 5, areas 8-13 inclusive), particularly the delta of the San Joaquin and Sacramento rivers, was entered relatively early by the Spaniards and by the year 1820 had been almost completely swept of its native population. The names of many whole tribes have been lost and the exact locations of many others are now almost impossible to ascertain. Of village names only those few are known to us which were preserved, often by chance, in the mission records and accounts of expeditions. Several attempts have been made to reconstruct the aboriginal human geography but none has been entirely successful. Kroeber's account, which accompanies his discussion of the Plains Miwok and northern Yokuts in the Handbook of California Indians, is manifestly incomplete. Merriam's paper on the Mewan Stock of California (1907) is helpful, but probably the best work of the modern investigators is that of Schenck (1926). The early nineteenth-century accounts for this region are also less satisfactory than for the central and southern parts of the San Joaquin Valley. Moraga's record is useful only for the Tuolumne River, and the delta is covered only by Abella and Duran. It is true that both Sutter and Gatten give figures for villages south of Sacramento but their information pertains only to the badly depleted natives of the 'forties. Hence their censuses are of little value for assessing the aboriginal condition.

One source not available for other areas is the mission records. The converts from the delta and lower San Joaquin Valley were brought almost exclusively into the San Francisco, San Jose, and Santa Clara missions. The baptism books of these missions have been preserved, and two copies have been made. The first, of the San Francisco Mission, was made by A. Pinart in 1878 and is at present in the Bancroft Library in Berkeley. The other records, copied by S. R. Clemence in 1919, include the records of all three missions and are now to be found, in typed form, among the manuscripts in the file of C. H. Merriam. The baptism books set forth the name and village of origin of every native in the mission, as well as the date of baptism. Newly converted gentiles are readily distinguished from infants born in the mission itself, since the origin of the latter is ascribed to the mission and not to a village. In addition to the names of villages, not all of which can be located with certainty, the dates of baptism constitute almost conclusive evidence. If the baptisms from San Francisco and Santa Clara are tabulated by village and date, it is very clear that the villages of local tribes were cleaned out before the year 1805. At this point an entirely new set of names appears, most of which are undoubtedly in the Tulares. Hence, if the name of a village does not correspond to any now known to ethnographers and no baptisms are reported from it prior to 1805, the conclusion is warranted that the village was actually situated in the central valley. The same assumption may be made with somewhat less certainty concerning the San Jose records. This mission was founded in 1797 and its earliest converts were drawn from the Costanoan tribes on the east shore of San Francisco Bay. The reduction of this region may not have been complete by 1805 and Tulare Indians were coming in by that year. Hence there is a chance of overlap. This source of error, however, may be excluded for all practical purposes if no doubtful village which continued to furnish converts after 1810 is included in the list, for the reduction of the Costanoans was certainly complete by that time.

Concerning village size various items of information are available. In the diary of Ramon Abella in 1811 he mentions that the Cholbones had three rancherias with a population of 900, or 300 per rancheria. That of the Coyboses had 180 and that of the Tauquimenes 200 men and 60 houses. The population of the latter tribe, if we apply the ratio found by Zalvidea at the southern end of the valley, should be 650. This ratio, it will be remembered, is based on Zalvidea's statement that he counted as men all males between the ages seven and forty. If, on the other hand, we assume that Abella referred to all males except small children and further that the sex ratio was unity, the adults would have numbered 400 and, if 15 per cent of the village were children, the total would be approximately 470. However, in the northern end of the valley we have much more solid data with which to work than at the extreme south.

The baptism records of the missions of San Jose and Santa Clara to which reference is made above include for each gentile village a breakdown of men, women, and children. These data have been already discussed in connection with the rancherias on Lake Tulare and it has been shown that, if proper correction is made for the sex ratio, men and women each contributed 41.8 per cent of the population and children 16.4 per cent. It is clear that in the north the Franciscans employed their standard system of calling children all persons under the age of ten years (not seven years) and including as males all men above the same age. Zalvidea's system was used only by himself. Consequently, a village with 200 men would have contained 563 persons in all.

For the village of the Tauquimenes with 60 houses the average would have been 9.38 persons per house. That this number is not excessive is demonstrated by the account of the village of Chuppumne contained also in Duran's diary. This rancheria had 35 houses, some of which were 40 to 50 paces in circumference. Since a pace is roughly a yard the diameter of such a house would be 43 feet, amply sufficient to accommodate 9 persons.

Chuppumne would thus have had a population of 315. Duran also mentions a rancheria of the Ochejamnes which had 40 houses, or 360 inhabitants.

Luís Argüello (MS, 1813) describes an expedition under the command of one Soto, whose party was attacked by Indians in the marshes of the delta. Schenck (1926, p. 129) locates the scene as in T5N, R4E, near Walnut Grove and designates the tribe as the Unsumnes or Cosumnes. Now Argüello states that the expedition crept up on the Indians overnight and attacked at dawn. They were surprised to find that their coming had nevertheless been detected and that the Indians had sent away the women and children. The Spaniards were met by a force of warriors, which Soto placed as his best estimate at 1,000 persons. These were drawn from four rancherias in the vicinity. One may always exercise skepticism with reference to these estimates of enemy forces, particularly in this instance, since the Spaniards were roughly handled and suffered several casualties in addition to being forced to withdraw. On the other hand, the invaders consisted of 13 well armed Spaniards and 100 Indian auxiliaries. Nothing like an equal number of natives could have withstood them. Soto's estimate may be cut in half but at least 500 warriors must be allowed, or 125 for each of the four rancherias. Now the fighting population, even in a great emergency, does not coincide with the total male population. If there were 500 warriors, there must have been fully 300 young boys, invalids, and old men who were not present. Hence we must concede a male population of no less than 800 for the four villages. If the percentage values established previously are used, the mean village size was approximately 475.

To the villages just described may be added the one seen by Moraga on the Stanislaus River in 1806, which had 200 inhabitants.

These twelve villages thus yield an average of 362 inhabitants each. Although throughout the territory many rancherias were doubtless small, it is equally probable that some were very large, approaching the magnitude of Chischa and Bubal in the south. Hence, unless in some particular instance there is clear reason to believe otherwise, 300 cannot be regarded as an excessive estimate for the average village of the delta.

In considering in detail the population of the delta (see map 6, area 13), it is convenient to segregate groups according to tribal distinctions rather than strictly according to geographical points. The reason lies primarily in the fact that the early writers and the mission records were relatively explicit with respect to names of villages and groups but were badly confused with respect to localities. In the densely populated but physiographically homogeneous delta region, with its scores of small streams, sloughs, and islands, explorers found it very difficult to establish clear landmarks by which the inhabitants might be oriented. A state of confusion has arisen of a kind to generate many controversies among ethnographers, controversies which are not pertinent in the present connection and which it is desirable to avoid as far as possible. In order to adopt a more or less uniform system with respect to tribal nomenclature and arrangement it is proposed to follow here the practice of Schenck (1926), who has made an exhaustive study of the area.

Bolbones (syn. Cholbones, Chilamne, Chulame).—This large group occupied the sloughs of the lower San Joaquin west of Stockton. Schenck, on his map (1926, p. 133) shows their territory as being bounded by the main stream of the San Joaquin River on the east and by the channel now known as the "Old River" on the west. This delineation of their habitat is supported by the diaries of Abella and Viader. Schenck classifies the subtribes or divisions of the main group as follows:

| Cholbones | a group |
| Pescadero | a village |
| Jusmites or Cosmistas | a village plus |
| Fugites or Tugites | a village plus |
| Tomchom, under Fugites | a village |
| Nototemnes | a village |

Although these natives are mentioned frequently in the correspondence of the period, the first recorded exploration of their area was that of Fr. José Viader in 1810. This missionary left Mission San Jose on August 15 and went by way of Pittsburg and Antioch to the mouth of the San Joaquin, whence he traveled southeast to Pescadero, "... la rancheria de los Cholvones." Leaving the rancheria he went on up the river. Viader's second expedition was carried out during the month of October of the same year. This time he went directly from San Jose to Pescadero, which he says was 15 leagues northeast to east-northeast of Mission San Jose. The account at this point is not particularly lucid. The entry for October 20 states that at Pescadero the gentiles were having a dance (bayle). That for the following day begins with the statement that at dawn Viader's party attacked "... asaltamos una rancheria de este lado del rio y solo escapo un Christiano ..." Then they attacked another rancheria on the other side of the river and captured 15 Christians and 69 gentiles. From the context it may be inferred that the first rancheria attacked was the one at which the dance was being celebrated on the evening of the 20th, that is to say, Pescadero. If it was, then there was another, quite sizable, village just across the river. If the first village was not Pescadero, then there were two other villages in close proximity to it.

The next visitor was Fr. Ramon Abella, who left San Francisco by boat on October 15, 1811. Passing Sherman Island on the 18th and wandering erratically through the swamps he reached the "tierra de los cholbones" on the next day. On October 20 he reached the village of Pescadero but made no comment on it in his diary. After examining the territory of the Cosmistas and Boyboses 5 to 15 miles to the east, the party turned about 8 to 9 miles (3 leagues) northwest, following the general trend of the river downstream. At this point they found a rancheria of 900 persons "divididas en tres rancherias, alguna distancia una de otras. No vimos que la una: Se presentan como 150 personas ... y nos enseñaron al desembarcadero y las mismas casas que havía duplicado gente ..." Abella's distances are extremely inaccurate but it is apparent that the three villages mentioned were north or northwest of Pescadero.

The key village in this complex is Pescadero, a rancheria to which repeated reference is made in the documents of the period and whose identity neither Viader nor Abella could have mistaken. That it belonged to the Bolbones is attested by Viader's expression "... la rancheria de los Cholvones." Viader saw at least one and perhaps two other villages near by belonging to the same tribe. Abella clearly states that he saw three rancherias in addition to Pescadero. One of these may have been the one attacked by Viader, and if so, the entire group included a minimum of four villages. Otherwise, there were at least five. Abella's count of 900 persons for the three villages appears accurate and reasonable. On the other hand, Pescadero was evidently regarded as the most important rancheria of the area and probably was more populous than any other. Hence it must have contained no less than 400 persons. The sum of the four villages would then be 1,300.

Between 1806 and 1811 the mission records show a total of 200 baptisms ascribed to the Cholbones, most of them at San Jose. In addition, there were 81 baptisms from 1821 to 1828 designated Chilamne. At the time of Abella's visit, therefore, the area had been subject to repeated raids for the purpose of securing converts and must have undergone serious social and economic disturbance of the type noted throughout the entire San Joaquin Valley. Merely adding the 200 missionized natives would bring the population estimate for the Bolbones up to 1,500, and the aboriginal value was probably even higher.

The Jusmites, or Cosmistas, are credited by Schenck with "a village plus," meaning certainly one and probably two or more. Viader, on his second expedition, found "los indios Jusmites" about 2½ leagues southeast of and up the river from the second village, which he attacked on October 21. This places them in the locality shown by Schenck on his map (1926,

p. 133), i.e., in northwestern T1S, R6E. No further information is given by Viader. The next year Abella found "la rancheria de los Cosmistas" in approximately the same region, but gave no data regarding size. Neither author implies in any way that there was more than one village. At San Jose 86 converts were baptized from "Jossmit," a number which suggests a village of fully 300 inhabitants.

Viader on his first expedition, on August 20, went south-southeast from Pescadero for 3 leagues and reached a village "cuyo capitan se llama Tomchom." He then went 2½ leagues southeast from the Jusmites and reached "los indios Tugites." Both Tomchom and Tugites therefore appear to have been in the same general area. For this reason Schenck has placed the Tugites, as a tribe, directly south of the Jusmites and has called Tomchom a village of the tribe. It is perhaps more likely that there were two villages involved (rather than a tribe and an included village), designated respectively Tomchom and Tugites. This view is substantiated by the baptism data. Of the entire group 268 were baptized, rather equally distributed between San Jose and Santa Clara. Over half the conversions occurred in the year 1811. The San Jose book lists 126 from "Tamcan" and 7 from "Tuguits." The Santa Clara book has 125 from "Los Tugites" and none under any other designation. It may therefore be concluded that two villages, or subtribes, were involved, one of which was taken to San Jose and the other to Santa Clara. A total of 268 converts would imply a population of at least 500 persons at the time of conversion and probably more aboriginally.

The village of Nototemnes is mentioned only by Duran in his diary of 1817. In the night of May 22-23 he passed "la rancheria de los Nototemnes," but did not actually see the village or count its inhabitants. However, the rancheria furnished 97 converts to Mission San Jose. It must therefore have contained at least 200 people. Schenck shows the Nototemnes as covering nearly two townships in the northern delta region and calls them "a village plus." He cites, however, no authority for this view other than Duran, and Duran, as mentioned above, refers only to the rancheria of the Nototemnes. There is no reason, consequently, for assuming more than one village for the tribe or group.

In summary, the Bolbones tribal complex consisted of fully eight medium to large villages. Those belonging to the Bolbones proper, four in number, were estimated to contain 1,500 persons. The Jusmites were allowed 300 persons, the Tugites 500, and the Nototemnes 200. The total is 2,500, and the average village size slightly over 300 persons.

(Bolbones ... 2,500)

Leuchas.—Schenck shows this tribe as living east of the San Joaquin River 10 to 15 miles south of Stockton. He implies that the tribe contained two villages, Coyboses and Pitemis (Aupimis), in addition perhaps to other settlements. The mission books mention all three names and show baptisms (figures in parentheses), which may be tabulated as follows.

|  | Baptisms, San Jose | Baptisms, Santa Clara |
| --- | --- | --- |
| Leuchas | "Leucha" (26), 1805-1812 (88 per cent in 1805-1806) | "Los Leuchas" (81), 1805-1809 (85 per cent in 1805) |
| Pitemis | None | (60), 1814-1831 (98 per cent in 1814-1816) |
| Coybos | (94), 1808-1826 (71 per cent in 1811-1812) | None |

To judge by the three separate periods in which the majority of the baptisms occurred there were three groups of people: the Leuchas, who were brought into the fold primarily during 1805 and 1806, the Coybos, principally in 1811-1812, and the Pitemis, converted two or three years later. The Leuchas were taken to both missions, but the Coybos were brought only to San Jose and the Pitemis only to Santa Clara. Abella said that in 1811 the village of Coybos had 180 inhabitants, a figure which has been used in computing the average village size. But the aboriginal population was probably greater. This view is substantiated by the events which preceded Abella's visit. In 1805 Father Cuevas of San Jose Mission went on an unauthorized expedition to the Leuchas—the best account is that by José Argüello (MS, 1805)—in search of converts.[5] He was badly treated and some of his men were wounded by the natives. This and the punitive expeditions which immediately followed no doubt accounted for the wave of conversions in 1805 and 1806. But at the same time the entire aboriginal group unquestionably suffered heavily from battle casualties and economic disturbance so that the population five years later must have been seriously reduced. It is thus justifiable to assume that originally there were three villages and that each was of average size. The population may therefore be set at fully 900 persons.

Some further information is derived from the recollections of José María Amador (MS, 1877). This pioneer, who received his facts second-hand from his father, mentions (pp. 13-15) the campaign of 1805 against the "Loechas," who, he says lived 4 to 5 leagues from Livermore. This would put them west of the San Joaquin River, south of the Bolbones, in T1S, R5E, not on the east bank as shown by Schenck. Amador then goes on to say that after the Cuevas affair the Leuchas "... se habian ya cambiado el rio de San Joaquin a una rancheria que se llamaba de los Pitemis." They were all captured and taken to San Jose. It is thus reasonably clear that the Leuchas originally did live west of the river, and crossed over to the east side as a result of the punitive expeditions of the Spaniards. Furthermore, the village of the Pitemis was already in existence at this time, probably at or near the spot shown by Schenck. Coybos undoubtedly was another village within the same area. This region, therefore, at the time of Abella's visit in 1807 contained the established villages of Pitemis and Coybos plus a residue of unconverted, fugitive Leuchas who had taken refuge in them.

Amador's assertion that the Leuchas were all captured and taken to San Jose is not borne out by the baptism figures, which show only 23 Leuchas enrolled at Mission San Jose in 1805 to 1806. Many more, actually 73, were baptized at Santa Clara in 1805. The total is 96, and scarcely represents the entire personnel of the group. Nevertheless, if we add the casualties of battle, disease, and exposure to those baptized in the missions, and allow for the dispersion of the remainder, the sum will amount to no less than the 300 assumed above for the Leuchas.

As for the Pitemis, Viader, on his first expedition, left Pescadero on August 20, 1810, and traveled south-southeast at some distance from the river. Within 3 leagues he passed "... en frente de una rancheria ... Aupemis." Schenck says (p. 141): "Pitemis is a village of the Leuchas and it seems that Aupimis is to be identified with it." This cannot be true because Viader is highly explicit to the effect that he was west of the river and Amador is equally emphatic in stating that Pitemis was across the San Joaquin from Leuchas, i.e., to the east of it. Since Viader's visit was in 1810, after the Cuevas affair, there must have been three rancherias of the Leuchas and their allies: Aupimis, Pitemis, and Coybos.

Parenthetically, and for the record, the present writer would like to offer the comment that certain modern writers tend to assert the identity of Spanish or Indian names without adequate evidence. Schenck's opinion that Aupimis and Pitemis were the same place could have been based upon no more than a fancied resemblance in the names. Also, of his paper he says: "The Leuchas might possibly be identified with Kroeber's Lakisamni (Yokuts) on the Stanislaus river." A brief examination of the mission records, apart from any other evidence, shows conclusively that two separate and distinct tribes were recognized by the contemporary missionaries.

(Leuchas et al. ... 900)

Ochejamnes.—This tribe is placed by Schenck on the east bank of the Sacramento River near the mouth of the Cosumnes. Kroeber refers to the village of Ochehak and considers it a "political community." He shows it on his map (1925, p. 446) as lying on the Mokelumne, due north of Stockton. Duran, in his diary, May 21 (MS, 1817), describes how he followed the main stream of the Sacramento, i.e., the left branch, on his way back from his stopping point above Courtland. He reached the rancheria "llamada de Oche jamnes," which, although it contained 40 houses, was deserted. Quite soon thereafter ("a poco rato") he reached "la punta de la isla llamada de los Quenemsias," which has been identified definitely as Grand Island. Clearly, therefore, in 1817 the Ochejamnes had a village on the Sacramento higher up the river than is shown by Schenck.

According to Duran the village had 40 houses, which would mean 360 persons without reckoning possible subsidiary rancherias. The name is mentioned for only one mission, San Jose, at which 428 Ochejamne, or Oocheganes, were baptized between 1829 and 1836. This is prima facie evidence that Duran, who saw them in 1817, was referring, as he implies, only to one rancheria and that the tribe was actually larger. This idea is supported by the account of José Berreyesa in 1830 of severe Indian fighting in the delta (Berryesa, MS, 1830). The Ochejamnes and the Yunisumnes with certain American trappers were arrayed against the Californians, who had gathered together 450 auxiliary fighters from the Cosumnes and other tribes. No value is placed upon the number of Ochejamnes but it must have been considerable. It was probably as a result of this campaign that 428 members of the tribe were baptized at Mission San Jose. Even with a relatively complete conquest many of the natives must have escaped; hence in 1830 their total number must have reached 500. But this was in 1830, after a generation of expeditions and petty warfare. The aboriginal number must have been considerably greater, let us say 750.

(Ochejamnes ... 750)

Guaypem.—This group is thought by Schenck to have been simply a village but Merriam (1907, p. 350) regards them as a tribe called the Wipa, located on Sherman Island near the Sacramento River estuary. Duran in his diary says that Guaypens is 6 leagues south and southeast of the fork of the river below Courtland. Allowing for his usual exaggeration of distances, this puts the rancheria near the mouth of the Mokelumne, in the vicinity of Walnut Grove. He speaks of the rancheria "de los Guaypens" and saw only a few people. Thus neither size nor locality supports the contention that Guaypem was synonymous with Wipa. The tribe was not converted until relatively late, 41 converts being taken to San Jose between 1821 and 1824. By that time the tribe had been subject to severe attrition. Thus the evidence points to an aboriginal group consisting of one village of average size, or close to 300 inhabitants.

(Guaypem ... 300)

Quenemsias.—These people, who lived near the two preceding tribes, are designated a "group" by Schenck (p. 136). They covered, according to him, "the southern part, or perhaps all, of Grand Island." The ecclesiastical diarists make no mention of them save the reference by Duran to the "isla llamada de los Quenemisias." One other citation is worth mentioning, however. In the Bancroft Transcripts is a document dated January 31, 1796, entitled "Informe en el cual el teniente Hermdo Sal manifesta lo que ha adquirido de varios sugetos para comunicarlo al Gobernador de la Provincia," which gives a description of the lower reaches of the San Joaquin and Sacramento rivers and the delta and mentions the natives (Sal, MS, 1796). In detail, the account is extremely inaccurate. However, one of the Indians "... dio noticia de las naciones Tulpunes, Quinensiat, Taunantoc, y Quisitoc: los primeros son de la orilla del estero; los 2os estan del otro lado de los rios ..." Although no numerical data are given, the mention of the Quenemsias (Quinensiat) as a "nacion" in the delta region establishes them as a group of more than average importance. The mission books show 185 Quenemsias baptized at Mission San Jose. Roughly double the number of baptisms may be taken as the aboriginal population, i.e., 400.

(Quenemsias ... 400)

Chuppumne, Chucumes.—Schenck places these two settlements, which he calls villages, on the Sacramento River near the mouth of the Cosumnes. Most of our documentary information concerning them is derived from the accounts of Duran and of Luís Argüello. Luís Antonio Argüello accompanied Duran on his expedition and wrote a report to the governor in the form of a letter, dated May 26, 1817, the original of which is preserved in the Bancroft Library (library no. fm-F864A64; also typed copy). The existence of this letter evidently was not known to either Kroeber or Schenck. It is less complete and less detailed than the diary of Duran but it is of value in checking the statements made by the latter.

On May 16 the party reached the foot of Grand Island and on May 17 proceeded up the left-hand (i.e., western) watercourse. The village of Chucumes was found 8 leagues (leguas) upstream, according to Duran, 13 miles (millas) according to Argüello. The latter estimate is probably closer, since Duran is notoriously inaccurate (usually on the side of overestimate) in his computation of distances. Here Duran counted 35 houses whereas Argüello says 36, a sufficiently close correspondence. As indicated previously, a population of 315 persons is probable. Continuing their journey, they went on for 4 miles (Argüello); Duran says approximately 3 leagues. There they stopped at a rancheria, "arruinada" according to Argüello, although Duran makes no mention of this.

On May 18 the party went on upstream, making during the day 4 leagues (Duran) or 16 miles (Argüello). Duran states that after going 1 league they got back into the main stream of the Sacramento. This was clearly at the head of Grand Island, close to Courtland. At 1 league beyond this point, on May 19, they found the rancheria Chuppumne, which was deserted. The location therefore was very close to that shown by Schenck on his map (p. 133) and, if we can put any credence in the Duran-Argüello account, a good many miles north of Chucumes. Near Chuppumne Duran saw three other rancherias in the distance (inland?) but could not get at them. On May 20 the expedition pressed on upstream for 5 miles (Argüello) or 4 leagues (Duran), at which point they turned around and began the return trip. On May 21 Argüello says that they passed "algunas rancherias," all deserted, which may well have been those mentioned by Duran on May 19.

On the river frontage covered from May 17 to May 21 the expedition saw a minimum of 6 villages, 2 of which are mentioned by name (Chucumes and Chuppumne) and for 1 of which the houses were counted. If all these villages were of comparable size—as they may have been aboriginally—then the total population represented would have been 1,800. This estimate would of course not include other villages which the expedition did not see.

The mission records show for San Jose a total of 377 persons baptized from Chucumne and Chuppumne, of whom 322 were converted during 1823 and 1824. We may predicate, therefore, a residual population of 700 to 800 just prior to those years. That the area had suffered severely before that is attested by the deserted and "ruined" rancherias seen by Duran in 1817. It is quite probable that the aboriginal population reached a value of 1,500.

(Chucumes, Chuppumne ... 1,500)

Chupunes (Chupcanes), Tarquines (Tarquimenes, Tauquines), Julpunes (Tulpunes) and Ompines.—This constellation of tribes is best considered collectively, first, because there are no direct estimates of their population, and second, because they occupied a relatively unified area.

Schenck places them along the south shore of Suisun Bay from the east entrance of Carquinez Strait and through the slough region between the Sacramento and San Joaquin rivers as far upstream as Isleton on the Sacramento. However, he points out that there is great uncertainty with respect to their exact location, an uncertainty which is emphasized by the wide divergence between his views and those of Merriam. Even the Spanish accounts present numerous discrepancies. In view of this state of our knowledge Schenck makes the very reasonable suggestion that the lower delta tribes may have been so greatly disturbed and shifted around during the period from 1775 to 1810 that the aboriginal locations were forgotten. It is worth while to examine in some detail some of the evidence on this problem. We may begin with examination of the area at and just east of Carquinez Strait on the south shore of Suisun Bay. This consideration entails a preliminary discussion of two small groups, the Aguastos and the Huchium (syn. Habastos, Quivastos, Juchium, Huchimes, Tuchimes, etc.).

This tribe or group of tribes, which must have been of some importance, is not mentioned by name by Kroeber or Schenck, but there is a brief set of typed notes in the Merriam collection in which the location is discussed (MS entitled: "On the East Side San Francisco Peninsula"). The multiplicity of synonyms, however, as well as the large number of neophytes involved, indicates that these tribes were very familiar to the missionaries.

The Merriam notes (pp. 5 and 6) point out the following considerations.

> 1. "Abella's diary (1811) speaks of present Point San Pablo as the Point of the Huchunes and says their territory extended on the mainland from this point to Pt. San Andres (Pt. Pinole)."

> 2. Several rancherias belonging to this tribe are mentioned as being on the east side of the bay.

> 3. "The mission books locate the Habasto tribe 'on the other side of the Bay from the Mission of San Francisco toward the estero which goes to the rivers (Suisun Bay).' Abella's diary calls Point San Pedro the Point of the Abastos."

Merriam therefore was strongly of the opinion that these tribes inhabited the south shore of San Pablo Bay and did not extend farther than Carquinez Strait.

On the other hand, the item in the mission books quoted by Merriam (par. 3, above) indicates Suisun Bay rather than San Pablo Bay. Moreover, there is another statement in the baptism books alongside the designation "Aguastos ó Huchum" to the effect that this tribe was 16 to 18 leagues by water from San Francisco. This distance would place them close to the site of the modern town of Pittsburg, that is, on the southern shore of Suisun Bay. But this area is assigned by Schenck to the Tarquines and perhaps the Julpunes, tribes which are also clearly mentioned by name in the mission records.

If the Aguastos extended from Richmond to Crockett or thereabouts, they were Costanoan and strictly bay people; hence not pertinent to this study. If they lived along Suisun Bay, regardless of their ethnic affiliation they may be included for demographic purposes among the delta tribes. Some further light can be thrown upon the problem by an analysis of the dates shown for baptisms in the San Francisco Mission records.

If the baptisms of gentiles are tabulated according to village and year, it is seen immediately that the conversions in the first year, 1777, were all from local rancherias. This group was extended during the following decade until the San Francisco peninsula had been completely covered. However, after the year 1792 all mention of the peninsula abruptly and entirely ceases. As early as 1778 on the other hand baptisms are listed from a village (Halchis) specified as being in the "sierra oriente de la otra banda." In the succeeding years villages ascribed to the "otra banda" become more frequent and reach a peak between 1790 and 1795. Subsequent to 1800 the conversions from these places diminish rapidly and disappear. Now we know by following the documentary accounts of expeditions that during the decade 1790 to 1800 the great effort of the San Francisco Mission was expended in securing neophytes from the east shore of San Francisco Bay as far north as the Carquinez Strait. There are no baptisms of gentiles whatever listed in the San Francisco books for the years 1797, 1798, and 1799. Therefore it is reasonable to assume that the supply of Costanoans from the east bay had been exhausted. Furthermore, village names qualified by the term "otra banda" and appearing in the baptism record for the first time prior to 1800 must certainly refer to villages in this region. Among these are rancherias stated as belonging to the "nacion Juchium" together with the separate designation "Tuchimes." Thus it is clear that the Huchium lived, as Merriam believed, on the east shore of the bay.

After the inactive period at the end of the century a flood of neophytes began to pour into the mission together with a completely new set of names. One of the first of these is Habastos, a rancheria which contributed 137 converts in 1800 and 1801 and which is now stated, for the first time in the mission book, to lie "acia el estero de los rios." Later, the variants Quivastos and Aguastos are used. Conversions from this tribe continued until 1810, after which the name disappears from the lists.

The sharp segregation of dates of conversion are clear evidence that, whatever the racial or linguistic affiliation, there were two groups of Indians, one converted before 1801 and living along the shore of the bay generally south and west of the Carquinez Strait, the other converted between 1801 and 1810 and living at the east end of the strait and along Suisun Bay. There probably was no clear separation of the two in the minds of the Spaniards; hence the confusion of names. We are concerned here with the second group, the one uniformly designated Aguastos, which inhabited the approaches to the delta.

With respect to the aboriginal population of this group we have no direct evidence whatever. On the other hand the record of the San Francisco Mission shows 396 baptisms. This immediately sets a lower limit to the number of Aguastos for there certainly can have been no fewer members of the tribe than were baptized. Regarding the upper limit it can be pointed out only that the group was completely obliterated at the time of conversion and its name never appears again in either contemporary or modern records. Hence it is safe to assume that substantially all the Aguastos were taken to San Francisco and that the baptisms include the entire tribe. We may thus ascribe to them a population of approximately 400 persons.

We now encounter the Chupunes (or Chupcanes), concerning whom Schenck (1926, p. 143) has this to say:

> The Chupunes (Chupcanes), apparently a group, were located along the southern shore near the east end of Carquinez strait. West of the strait, also on the southern shore—in the Pinole region of San Pablo bay—were the Huchones.

The earliest documentary reference is to the diary of Abella, in 1811. On October 16 he went through Carquinez Strait by boat. Then he says that the strait "... remata en la tierra de los Chupunes, porque hay ya ensancha ..." The "ensancha" or widening begins at Port Costa and continues to Martinez. This, then, is the boundary of the Chupunes. On October 28, discussing the Suisunes on the north side of the bay, he says that "La rancheria citada de los Suisunes cahe al nordeste de los Chupanes, tierra adentro del Cerro de los Karquines ..." The Cerro de los Karquines is, of course, Mt. Diablo.

In his account of the expedition of 1817 Duran tells how he arrived at noon of May 14, by boat from San Francisco, at the "remate" of the "estrecho de los Chucanes," at a point 14 leagues northeast of San Francisco and 17 leagues north-northeast of San Jose. The rancheria of this name, he states, is now Christian, at San Francisco and San Jose. The mission books show a total of 105 baptisms at the two establishments.

It is reasonably plain that the Aguastos and the Chupunes occupied more or less the same territory—along the south shore of the eastern end of Carquinez Strait and the western end of Suisun Bay. The diaries and the baptism records both indicate that the original inhabitants were the Aguastos, who were missionized and removed. Their place seems to have been taken by another group of natives known as the Chupunes, who also were gathered into the fold at some period between the visits of Abella and Duran. Subsequent to the 1817 diary of Duran there is no further mention of this tribe. With respect to population we have only the record showing 105 baptisms. Since the conversion seems to have been quite complete, we may set the aboriginal value at no more than 150.

Let us now consider the Ompines. This group is placed by Schenck on the north bank of the Sacramento River at and above the junction of the river and Suisun Bay. Schenck also (p. 137) discusses the possibility that the Ompines and Julpunes composed a single group. In spite of an assumed similarity in names the Spanish accounts are unequivocally explicit to the effect that there were two groups, not one, hence Schenck's hypothesis may be disregarded. With respect to location the later Spanish accounts bear out Schenck's contention that the tribe was situated north of the river.

In his entry for May 14, 1817, Duran says that his expedition stopped at the mouth of the San Joaquin River, whereas another boat (that of Argüello) stopped opposite "en tierra de Ompines." The next day they all went up the Sacramento River to the "remate de las lomas de los Ompines." Meanwhile Argüello, in his entry for May 15, says that they went along the north shore and stopped "donde termina la tierra de los Ompines." This puts the eastern edge of the Ompines at the east side of the Montezuma Hills in T3N, R2E, approximately as shown by Schenck. Altimira describes an unauthorized raid by Fr. Duran on the tribes north of Suisun Bay, among them "... otra rancheria aislada llamada los Ompines" (Altimira, MS, 1823).

A few of the earlier documents, on the other hand, contain statements which raise the possibility that the Ompines were not always confined exclusively to the north shore. In his diary of 1811 Abella describes how, on October 17, his party entered a big bay (Suisun Bay) and, after 5 leagues, following along the south shore, began to find estuaries and numerous islands covered with tules. They continued into the west channel of the San Joaquin and stopped at an island on which large trees were growing. At this point, somewhere near Antioch, there was a "pescadero" of the Ompines. It is evident, therefore, that in 1811 the Ompines had at least temporary fishing spots on the south side of the estuary, in an area usually ascribed to the Julpunes or Tarquines.

The San Jose baptism book shows the conversion of 108 Ompines. Those from San Rafael and Solano do not mention the tribe. The fact that a tribe situated north of Suisun Bay does not appear in the records of either of these missions is noteworthy, since during the 1820's and 1830's the north-bay groups were brought to them in large numbers, and since we know from Altimira's comment on Duran's raid that the Ompines were still in existence in 1823. Furthermore, the Ompines must have constituted more than a single small village, for Argüello and Duran both refer to the "tierra" of the Ompines. The hypothesis is possible, although admittedly there is no real proof, that the Ompines may have originally occupied the sloughs and islands at and above Antioch, that they may have been pushed north at an early date by Spanish intrusion from the south and west, and that they may have been further dispersed, or exterminated without extensive conversion, prior to 1830. If such a theory in any way represents the course of their decline and disappearance, then it also follows that the aboriginal population was considerably greater than the baptism number would lead one to suppose.

To turn now to the Julpunes, there seems to be little difference of opinion regarding their original location. This was as Schenck pictures it: the south shore of the San Joaquin estuary from Antioch to the line between R3E and R4E. The "Informe" of Hermengildo Sal, written in 1796 and previously referred to, specifies the "Tulpunes" as a "nacion" living on the "orilla del estero." Fourteen years later in 1810 Viader went 7 leagues from Pittsburg to the "old river" west of Stockton. He was: "... esta tierra es de los Tulpunes." Duran, May 24, 1817, on his return journey downstream reached the region of the Julpunes at 8:00 A.M. and joined the other boat at 6:00 P.M. of the same day at Carquinez Strait.

Schenck (1926, p. 137) points out that Kotzebue, who was in the area in 1823, implies that the Julpunes were living on the north bank. Merriam (1907, p. 348), says that the Hulpoomne "occupied the east bank of the Sacramento River from a few miles south of the mouth of American river southward ..." Schenck's explanation of the discrepancy appears to the present writer entirely sound: the Julpunes retired across the estuary to the north bank and then upstream nearly to Sacramento. In so doing they may very well have carried the surviving Ompines with them. The San Jose record lists 148 baptisms of Julpunes but the name is absent from the records of San Francisco, Santa Clara, San Rafael, and Solano missions. Along with the Ompines the Julpunes must have escaped the active proselyting effort of San Rafael, and particularly Solano, between 1824 and 1834, by a rapid retirement so far up the river as to elude the parties sent out from the missions. The converts at San Jose must have been captured by the Viader, Duran, Argüello, and similar expeditions before the migration upstream.

The Tarquines are claimed by Schenck to have been "... a single group. It seems to have stretched from east to west entirely across the marsh area between the main channels of the Sacramento and San Joaquin rivers, and then to have extended along the southern shore of Suisun Bay" (pp. 134-

136). Schenck's belief in this remarkable distribution is based upon three documentary references (at least he cites no more than these three in his tabulation on p. 135).

The first of the three documents, chronologically, is the first expedition of Viader, in 1810. In his entry for August 17 Viader says that, having spent the preceding night near the present location of Pittsburg, he reconnoitred these lands which "... son de los Tarquines, que lo mas, 6 casi todos son Cristianos de San Francisco." After noting the mouths of the two rivers, he goes on to mention a spot on the estuary "... en donde dicen estaba la rancheria de los Tarquines" (emphasis mine). Let it be emphasized that in 1810 the Tarquines are almost all Christians in San Francisco, and Viader saw there the rancheria which was, or had been, that of the Tarquines. The San Francisco baptism book shows 18 "Talquines" converted in 1801 and 63 more in 1802, making a total of 83. This number could well be the majority, or almost all, the inhabitants of a moderate-sized rancheria. Schenck is therefore technically correct in placing the tribe on the south shore of the eastern end of Suisun Bay.

The second document is the diary of Abella in 1811. On October 25, in the course of the return trip downstream, some distance below the junction of the channels of the San Joaquin, he found a rancheria of the Tauquimenes, one part of each side of the river, which was 30 to 40 varas wide. This point was apparently at or near the head of Sherman Island. The rancheria had 60 houses. He saw 200 warriors. He then crossed through the sloughs to the Sacramento River and on or opposite Sherman Island saw one rancheria of 14 houses and several of 2 to 3 houses. He says that all they passed this day was "... parte de una isla" (i.e., Sherman Island). Furthermore

> ... en todo este dia andubimos como unas 12 leguas [overestimate] y podra haver gente, como 200 almas, todavia puede que haiga mas, porque en la primera [rancheria] habraumas 1,000, segun lo grande que por aqui son las casas, tienen un circuito de 28 o 30 varas, con su orcon en medio ...

This account deserves comment on several grounds: with relation to Viader's visit of the previous year and the baptisms at San Francisco it is evident that whereas the southern extension of the Tarquines' habitat, whatever its size, had been swept clear prior to 1810, nevertheless the tribe persisted on the estuarine islands in truly large numbers. Moreover, since there is evidence of no more than one rancheria on the south shore, it appears that the territory in that region allotted by Schenck to the tribe is too large and should be restricted to a small area of the southeastern corner of Suisun Bay.

With respect to population, Abella's figures are quite credible. It has been suggested that one of the huge houses found in this region could accommodate 9 persons without difficulty. Then the large village should have had 540 inhabitants. Allowing 24 houses for the other villages seen, 216 persons should be added, making a total of 756, a figure not far from Abella's guess of 1,000.

The final reference to the tribe occurs in the diary of Duran. During the night of May 22-23, 1817, he went up the main channel of the San Joaquin, in T3N, R4E, and passed the Tauguimenes on the left, that is to say, on the east bank. Schenck thinks that the group covered the entire strip from Pittsburg to the east bank of the main river contemporaneously. Now it has been pointed out as probable that the southwestern outliers were missionized, or pushed back into the swamps, as early as 1801. It is equally possible that the island communities described by Abella in 1811 were pushed, in the next five or six years, off the islands altogether and clear back eastward to the far bank of the main river. Of considerable significance is the fact that whereas both Viader and Abella mention the Tarquines as being in the estuary region, Duran, who covered this area thoroughly, is completely silent with regard to their presence. It is highly unlikely that, had there been any of the tribe left in their former habitat, he would have failed to note them.

The details are very obscure but the main outlines of events in the first three decades of the nineteenth century can be perceived. Aboriginally and perhaps till nearly 1800, there was a dense population of natives extending from Port Costa along the southern shore of Suisun Bay and up the rivers for fifteen miles beyond Antioch. Among them were included tribal groups, or rancherias, called Aguastos, Chupunes, Ompines, Julpunes, and Tarquines, belonging very likely to different ethnic and linguistic stocks. Under the pressure of the Spanish military power, which was the real force behind missionization, portions of these groups were exterminated, other segments gave ground and shifted habitat, and occasional remnants persisted in the old localities. Thus each visitor in turn found a different geographical organization, until the entire native society was obliterated.

An accurate assessment of aboriginal population in this area is impossible. The best we can do is try to make an intelligent guess. Several methods are available for this purpose—group comparisons, mission figures, area comparisons.

Throughout the plains of the lower San Joaquin and Sacramento valleys the native social units appear to have resembled rather uniformly the political organization of the Yokuts in the central and southern San Joaquin

Valley. There were aggregates, or communities, consisting of perhaps one, but usually more than one, village, and occupying a more or less clearly defined territory. These groups, as they may be called, can be identified by the plural names which are ordinarily attached to them—the Bolbones, the Leuchas, and so forth. Naturally these groups varied considerably in size, and concerning no single one of them can we be absolutely sure of the number of their people. Nevertheless, if we had data concerning enough of them, the variations due both to inherent difference and to inaccurate estimate would tend to cancel out and an approximate average could be secured. No pretence can be made that we have enough estimates to establish a mean which would be statistically satisfactory. Nevertheless, as so frequently happens when we are dealing with data of this character, we have to employ the information available to us or forsake the problem entirely.

We have hitherto considered a number of the local groups mentioned above and have estimated their population as follows: Bolbones (restricted group, see p. 58), 1,500; Jusmites, 300; Tugites, 500; Nototemnes, 200; Leuchas, 900; Ochejamnes, 750; Guaypem, 300; Quenemsias, 400; Chucumes and Chuppumne, 1,500. The average for the nine groups is 705 or, in round numbers, 700. If we consider that the Aguastos, Chupunes, Ompines, Julpunes, and Tarquines were groups of the same character as the foregoing, then their total population may be taken as 3,500.

The total baptisms shown in the mission books of the five northern missions (in fact, only San Francisco and San Jose) for these groups is 911. In previous instances we have estimated the aboriginal population by doubling the baptism number. This procedure is admittedly purely arbitrary and based upon the general consideration that, except for small local populations relatively close to the mission, it was impossible for the missionaries and soldiers to prevent the escape of a sizable fraction of the people. Of the five groups here discussed, the Aguastos, it is evident, were completely missionized or at least obliterated. A much greater proportion of the other tribes survived, as is attested by their probable migrations up the rivers. Hence for the entire population it is doubtful if even one-half received baptism. Using the value of one half, the aboriginal number would have been approximately 2,000.

Linear distances along streams are useful as a basis for comparison in country where the rivers are similar ecologically but are clearly separated spatially and where the human population is concentrated along the stream banks to the exclusion of the interfluvial hinterland. Where a territory is marked by a network of creeks and sloughs, and the intermediate land is marsh, the linear comparisons become impossible. Areas must be substituted.

In relation to the present problem three such areas may be delineated. The first comprises the territory of the Bolbones (including all the subordinate villages) and the Leuchas. Following Schenck's map, it embraces all the land between the channels of the San Joaquin plus a strip approximately two miles wide east of the main river in T1 and 2S, R6E which accounts for the Leuchas. The area, as projected from a large-scale map onto coördinate paper, is 775 square miles, the population 3,400, and the density 4.39 persons per square mile. The second comprises the home of the Ochejamnes, Guaypem, Quenemsias, and Chucumnes-Chuppumne. For the habitat of these groups we have followed Schenck as far as possible. Our line runs actually from the junction of the east and west channels of the Sacramento at the foot of Grand Island southeast to the main channel of the San Joaquin, thence northeast and north to just east of Walnut Grove and then, at a distance of about 2 miles east of the eastern channel of the Sacramento, to a point 4 miles north of Courtland. Here the line crosses the river and continues downstream, 2 miles west of the river, to the starting point. This strip of the western bank of the western branch of the Sacramento is included in order to take in the Chucumes, who may have lived on the west side of the river. The area of this territory is 330 square miles, the population 2,950, and the density 8.94 persons per square mile.

The third area is the one shown by Schenck as belonging to the Chupunes, Tarquines, Julpunes, and Ompines, with the exception of the region east of the San Joaquin attributed to the Tarquines. For reasons stated previously the author does not believe that the Tarquines occupied this spot aboriginally. A strip 2 miles wide is included on the north shore, however, between Rio Vista and Collinsville, in the probable land of the Ompines. The eastern boundary is formed by the borders of areas one and two. In area three there are 600 square miles. The mean of the densities of the other two areas is 6.67 persons per square mile. Hence the population would have been 4,002 persons. No significance should be attributed to the third and probably also the second digit in these numbers. They are used only for purposes of estimate.

The three methods employed have yielded respectively 3,000, 2,000, and 4,000 as the most likely population of the five groups here being discussed. In default of any other evidence we may take the average 3,000.

(Chupunes, Tarquines, Ompines, Julpunes ... 3,000)

Adding the totals for the tribes known to inhabit the delta region of the great rivers and the southern shore of Suisun Bay, we arrive at a total population of 9,350.

Delta area ... 9,350

It is now preferable to depart from a strictly tribal sequence and revert once more to a classification based upon river basins. Three areas of this type are sufficiently clearly marked out; those corresponding to (1) the Cosumnes River, (2) the Mokelumne River, and (3) the lower San Joaquin River from just below the Merced to the head of tide water near Manteca. The inhabitants may be designated village or tribal groups in accordance with the river system where they were located.

The Cosumnes group.—On the river of this name lived the large and important aggregate of peoples known popularly as the Cosumnes, which included a restricted tribelet or subgroup also called Cosumnes. Ethnically a portion of the Plains Miwok, they extended from Sloughhouse close to the foothills, along the lower course of the Cosumnes River to its confluence with the Mokelumne near Thornton, and from that point northwestward to the Sacramento. The tribe as a whole was divided into either villages or tribelets, the names of many of which have come down to us from the Spanish records or have been ascertained by informants from ethnographers. As might be expected, there is considerable confusion among the different sets of names.

The mission documents are replete with village and tribal names but the number of baptisms was not as large as might be anticipated from what must have been a very populous aggregate of natives. The reason probably lies in the fact that missionizing expeditions to the Cosumnes were preceded by exploratory and punitive expeditions which, to be sure, brought home a few converts but which were chiefly preoccupied with military objectives. The Cosumnes, together with the Mokelumnes and other peoples of the lower San Joaquin Valley, had the time and the opportunity to develop great facility in the raiding and stealing of livestock and consequently for many years were in a state of uninterrupted war with the coastal settlers. The bitter hostility thus generated, together with the aggressive psychology which accompanied successful physical opposition to the Spaniards, made extensive conversion to Christianity very difficult. As a result the relative proportion of the natives baptized was unquestionably much lower than among the bay and delta tribes previously considered. The baptisms which appear in the mission records follow.

| Tribe or Group | Date of Conversion | Baptisms |
|---|---|---|
| Cosumnes (Tribelet) | 1826-1836 | 84 |
| Junisumne (Anizumne, Unsumne) | 1813-1834 | 363 |
| Lelamne (Llamne) | 1813-1836 | 128 |
| Gualacomne | 1825-1836 | 158 |
| Amuchamne (Mackemne) | 1834-1835 | 13 |
| Sololumne | 1828-1834 | 6 |
| Locolumne | 1826-1834 | 52 |
| Total | | 804 |

If we apply the general principle used with the delta groups and double the baptism number, the population becomes 1,608, a figure which is much too low. The Lelamne, with 128 baptisms, comprises the group attacked by Soto in 1813, at which time we have estimated that there were four villages of 475 persons each involved in the battle. This calculation implies a total of 1,900 for the Lelamne alone. On the other hand, the account is not entirely clear as to whether or not there were members of the Cosumnes tribelet concerned. If so, we may be dealing with both the Lelamne and adjacent neighbors who were designated locally Cosumnes. If we include the baptisms of all those under both names, we have 212. Furthermore, the Junisumne (or Unsumne or Anizumne) were often confused with the Cosumnes. If the 363 baptisms listed under the Junisumne are added we get 575 and, multiplying by 2, the population of the three divisions collectively would have been 1,150. This estimate also appears too small and leads to the conclusion suggested above on historical grounds that a baptism factor valid for the delta would not be applicable to the Cosumnes group as a whole.

Another documentary source is of interest in this connection. This is the account by José Berreyesa in 1830 (MS) of an affray along the lower Sacramento River in which Americans participated under Ewing Young. Christian fugitives from the missions had been protected by the Yunisumenes (Junisumne), who had joined with the Ochejamnes. They were opposed by the Mexicans and their allies, the Sigousamenes (Siakumne), the Cosomes, and the Ilamenes. These last tribes had gathered an army of 450 "Gentiles auciliares." The Yunisumenes, Cosomes, and Ilamenes are, of course, precisely the three subtribes discussed in the preceding paragraph. Now if the Sigousamenes, Cosomes, and Ilamenes contributed 450 men collectively, they each may be considered to have furnished 150 men. Since the opponents were fairly well matched, it is likely that the Yunisumenes supplied a similar number. We can assume that for routine fighting of this sort, particularly where two of the tribelets were ranged with the Mexicans instead of against them, the armies included no more than the strictly military population, or not in excess of half the males over the age of ten years. Hence, if the sex ratio was unity and the young children constituted approximately 15 per cent of the population, the aggregate number of the three subtribes would have amounted to 1,920, or almost the same as was estimated from the Soto report in 1813 for the Lelamne (Ilamenes) above, or perhaps the Lelamne augmented by some of the Cosumnes tribelets or subtribes. The Berreyesa episode occurred in 1830, after all these groups had suffered twenty years of attrition owing to perpetual minor warfare, disease, and starvation. Hence the population of the three tribelets jointly, Junisumne, Cosumnes, and Lelamne, must have reached fully 3,000 in 1813. The baptism factor, consequently, would not have been 50 per cent, but 575 divided by 3,000, or 19.2 per cent.

Three other villages or tribelets which can be identified in the mission records as being closely associated with the Cosumnes are the Amuchamne, Sololumne, and Locolumne. The first two probably correspond to Merriam's Oo-moo-chah and So-lo-lo, which in later times at least were rancherias. Assuming all three to have been villages, we may consider that each contained an average number of 300 inhabitants. The respective baptism numbers were 13.6, and 52. In relative terms the baptisms amounted to 4.3, 2.0, and 17.3 per cent.

The last division listed above is the Gualacomne, synonymous with Merriam's Wah-lah-kum-ne. Merriam (Mewko List, MS) places them between the lower Stanislaus and the Tuolumne rivers, but quotes Hale, who saw them in the 1840's, as saying that they lived on the lower east side of the Sacramento River. Hale's statement is strongly supported by the fact that they appear in J. A. Gatten's census of 1846 (MS, 1872). Gatten ennumerated only the tribes along the lower Sacramento. Whether the Gualacomne can be affiliated with the Cosumnes ethnically is doubtful but it is reasonable to include them with this group demographically.

Of the Gualacomne 158 were baptized in the missions. That the group was fairly large is attested by the fact that Gatten reported, under the name Yalesumne, that 485 were alive in 1846, Since no open valley group could possibly have retained more than one-third of its former members in 1846, it does not seem excessive to ascribe 1,455 persons to the tribelet. The baptism factor is 10.8 per cent, and the average of the five values secured with the Cosumnes group is 10.7, or, let us say 10.0 per cent. The total population on the lower Cosumnes and adjacent Sacramento rivers, according to the discussion above would be 5,355 souls.

We may approach the problem from a different direction if we start with the villages compiled by Merriam (1907, p. 349). He mentions sixteen villages on the Cosumnes River system from Sloughhouse nearly but not quite to the Sacramento. It is extremely probable that there were other villages on the Sacramento River itself. Nevertheless, let us take Merriam's list as it stands. The upper seven villages lie between Sloughhouse and the junction of the Cosumnes River with Deer Creek, the remainder below that point. Of the lower nine we may consider that four correspond to those seen by Soto, which were quite large. It was estimated that they contained 475 persons apiece. The other five lower villages, although perhaps not so populous, must have held fully 300 inhabitants each. The upper seven were no doubt smaller but still should have reached the values given by Moraga for similar stretches of the Tuolumne and Merced, i.e., approximately 250 persons. The total would then come to 5,150, very close to the previous estimate. It will be both adequate and conservative to establish the population at 5,200.

Cosumnes group ... 5,200

The Moquelumne group.—Here are included the Indians living on the lower course of the Mokelumne River, the Calaveras River, and the plain between the two. Five tribes mentioned by the Spanish writers fall within this category: the Moquelumnes, the Siakumne, the Passasimas, the Yatchikumne and the Seguamne. The exact territorial status of these tribes has been a subject of considerable disagreement among ethnographers.

The original Moquelumnes of the Spaniards were undoubtedly located on the Mokelumne River itself from Campo Seco nearly to the junction with the Cosumnes at which point they adjoined the Cosumnes tribe. According to George H. Tinkham, in his History of San Joaquin County (1923), they extended in a north-south direction all the way from Dry Creek to the Calaveras River, but by the middle of the nineteenth century they may have spread out from their original habitat. The Yatchikumne are shown by Schenck as filling the space between the lower Mokelumne and the lower Calaveras and extending westward to the San Joaquin River. Merriam (Mewko List, MS) quotes F. T. Gilbert to the effect that they occupied the Mokelumne River basin, but if they did so, it was because of the displacements during the mining era. The Passasimas are placed by

Schenck on the left bank of the Calaveras River at, and for several miles upstream from, its junction with the San Joaquin River.

The Siakumne and the Seguamne are subject to some confusion. This difficulty arises partially from the similarity in name. The Siakumne are called Si-a-kum-ne by Merriam and Sakayakumne by Kroeber. In Gatten's census of 1846 they appear as Sagayakumne. In the San Jose baptism book we find Ssicomne, Zicomne, Siusumne, and Sigisumne. The Seguamne, on the other hand are designated Seguamnes and Saywamines by Merriam and Sywameney or Seywameney by Sutter in his New Helvetia Diary (1939). Gatten calls them Sywamney. They appear in the San Jose record as Secuamne, Seguamne, Seyuame, and other variants.

The Siakumne lived somewhere between the Calaveras and Stanislaus rivers according to Merriam, who places one of their villages at Knights Ferry on the Stanislaus. Schenck doubts Merriam's location and Kroeber puts the rancheria Sakayakumne as far north as the Mokelumne. Sutter (1939, p. 88) says that some of these people came to work for him, an unlikely event if they had been living as far away as the Stanislaus. It is probable that the lower Calaveras River is as close as we can place them. The Seguamne are not mentioned at all by Schenck. Merriam (Mewko List, MS) says they were a "tribe or subtribe on E. side lower Sacramento River" and may have been a subtribe of the Bolbones. Sutter and Gatten both refer to the tribe, and the sphere of activity of these men did not extend much below the Sacramento River itself. Hence, although there are grounds for including the Seguamne with the Bolbones or the Cosumnes, no serious error will be committed by placing them in the Mokelumne group.

The Moquelumnes were unquestionably quite numerous. In Spanish and Mexican times they were the most aggressive and belligerent of all the valley tribes and gave the coastal settlers a very rough struggle. Nevertheless, in spite of their detestation of the missionaries they furnished 143 converts between 1817 and 1835. At a ratio of 10 per cent this would mean a population, prior to the mission period, of about 1,400 souls. J. M. Amador (MS, 1877, p. 43) says that once, during the later colonial period, they furnished 200 auxiliaries, a fact which would argue fully 1,000 people at the time. Gatten in his census of 1846 gives them a total of 81 persons but G. H. Tinkham says that in 1850 or thereabouts they possessed four sizable villages with four chieftains. This may have meant between 200 and 400 persons, a really considerable number of survivors for a tribe which had suffered so extensively in the preceding three decades. These indications, and it must be admitted that they are only indications, would lead one to infer that the aboriginal population reached at least 1,500.

Precisely because the Moquelumnes were so brutally handled in the colonial era the modern ethnographic accounts of villages are very incomplete. Neither Merriam nor Schenck gives us any list. Kroeber puts three on his map (1925, opp. p. 446): Mokel (-umni), Lelamni, and Sakayak-umni. I think we are now in a position to state that these names represent former tribes and if they were applied to villages by informants, it is because the component units had shrunk to very small size.

Stream density comparisons are of value for the Mokelumne group. On the Cosumnes River, from Sloughhouse to Thornton, Merriam shows thirteen rancherias (omitting those close to the Sacramento River). As was proposed above we may ascribe from 200 to 400 inhabitants to each of these, say on the average 300. Now there is no reason to suppose that the Mokelumne River from the San Joaquin-Calaveras county line to just west of Lodi was less heavily populated than the Cosumnes. If so, the number of villages per linear river mile must have been very nearly the same. For the stretches under consideration there were 24 miles on the Cosumnes and 22 on the Mokelumne. Thus we would get 12 villages and 3,600 persons living on the Mokelumne River.

The Yatchikumne and, if we are to credit Schenck, the Passasimas occupied a position on the Calaveras River comparable to that occupied by the Moquelumnes on the Mokelumne. Schenck regards the Yatchikumne as a tribe equal in importance to the Moquelumnes, and the county historians speak of them as a large group. Their river frontage is equivalent to that of the Moquelumnes. For these reasons we would be justified in ascribing to the Yatchikumne and Passasimas the same population as the Moquelumnes, i.e., 3,600. The evaluation of the other two groups from the geographical standpoint is difficult, owing to the uncertainty of their location. The Siakumne may be regarded as living somewhere on the lower Calaveras and, if so, must be included with the Yatchikumne and Passasimas in the estimate for the Calaveras. The Seguamne may or may not have inhabited the banks of the Mokelumne and Calaveras rivers. In view of our ignorance on this point it may be well to omit them from consideration in this connection and leave the estimate with the existing total of 7,200.

We may attempt some direct tribal comparisons. In considering the northern San Joaquin Valley and delta 21 tribes and tribelets have been examined, namely: Aguastos, Bolbones (4 tribes), Leuchas, Ochejamnes, Guaypen, Quenemsias, Chuppumne, Chupunes, Tarquines, Julpunes, Ompines, and the Cosumnes group (7 tribes). For all these the average population calculated has been very close to 700. If this figure is applied directly to the Moquelumne group, its population becomes 3,500. However, some adjustment is necessary. The Moquelumnes by all accounts, Spanish and American, were an unusually large tribe, probably reaching at least 1,500. The Yatchikumne may not have been as numerous but were apparently above the average size, let us say 1,200. The Passasimas, despite the fact that Schenck thinks they were a "group plus" may be regarded as smaller, perhaps no more than average. For the Siakumne and Seguamne we must also assume the average figure, 700. With these adjustments the total reaches 4,800.

The baptism books give us a record of the following conversions.

| Tribe | San Jose | Santa Clara |
| --- | --- | --- |
| Moquelumnes | 143 | ... |
| Yatchikumnes | 118 | ... |
| Passasimas | 145 | ... |
| Siakumne | 22 | ... |
| Seguamne | 47 | 116 |

The Passasimas, Siakumne, and Seguamne were situated in the vicinity of the San Joaquin River and hence were more exposed to the Spanish expeditions than the tribes along the lateral streams. Hence the proportion of those taken for conversion may have been higher than the 10 per cent of the aboriginal population found for the Cosumnes, although it would not have attained the value of 50 per cent characteristic of the more westerly delta tribes. We may take an intermediate figure, 20 per cent. This would give the Passasimas a population of 725, the Siakumne 110, and the Seguamne 815. The great disparity between the figures for the last two tribes may well be due to confusion of names in the mission records. The total for the three is 1,650. For the Yatchikumne on the Calaveras River no more than 10 per cent baptisms can be assumed, yielding a population figure of 1,180. If only geographical location were considered, the same factor could be used for the Moquelumnes but this tribe resisted missionization with extraordinary tenacity. Hence we are not justified in using a factor of more than 7 per cent, from which we may infer that the population was 2,040. The baptism data would then give us a total for the group of 4,870.

According to the estimates furnished by pioneers and government officials for the period just preceding the Gold Rush the population ran into the thousands. The census by Savage (Dixon, MS, 1875) puts 4,000 on the Cosumnes, Mokelumne, and Calaveras and 2,500 on the Stanislaus, F. T. Gilbert (1879, p. 13) says that "before the advent of Sutter" there were 2,000 on the Mokelumne and, as far as I can ascertain, he implies that on the Cosumnes and Mokelumne together there were fully 5,000. These figures were undoubtedly greatly exaggerated but nevertheless indicate a very large population in the area just before the discovery of gold and subsequent to the destructive epidemics of 1833-1835. Even if we cut these estimates in half, there would remain in midcentury approximately 2,000 persons in the basins of the Moquelumne, Calaveras, and adjacent San Joaquin rivers. A residue of 2,000 in 1850 means certainly an original population of three times as much, i.e., 6,000.

To recapitulate the estimates for the Moquelumne group, we find:

| | |
|---|---|
| By stream densities | 7,200 |
| By adjusted tribal averages | 4,800 |
| By baptism data | 4,870 |
| By extrapolation from American estimates | 6,000 |
| Mean | 5,720 |

The mean, 5,720, appears entirely reasonable for the aboriginal population of such a vigorous and important group.

Moquelumne group ... 5,720

The lower San Joaquin River group. —Here are included for convenience the tribes and fragments of tribes inhabiting the banks of the San Joaquin River from the habitat of the Leuchas, in the vicinity of Manteca, to just below the mouth of the Merced, together with those living along the lower courses of the Stanislaus and Tuolumne rivers (see maps 1, 5, and 6, area 8). The San Joaquin villages or tribes appear to have been Cuyens, Mayemes, Tationes, and Apaglamnes. The first two are regarded by Schenck as villages only and the latter two as "villages plus." The only Spaniard who described the area was Viader, in the accounts of his two expeditions of 1810.

On his first expedition, having left the village of Tomchom, he went south-southeast up the river for 2½ leagues to another village "... cuya capitan se llama Cuyens." This was very close to section 10, in T3S, R6E. After a journey of another 2½ to 3 leagues he found another village, whose captain was Maijem (sec. 8, in T4S, R7E). Then, after 2 leagues, still another village, whose captain was Bozenats (in sec. 34, in T4S, R7E), was seen. Three leagues farther in the same direction brought him to the rancheria "... cuyo appelido es Tationes." In the meantime he had seen 30 gentiles from the Apaglamnes. The Tationes were located close to section 27, in T5S, R8E.

During his second expedition, on October 22, Viader went from Pescadero southeast up the river for 5 leagues to "los indios Tugites." Three leagues farther on he was met by Indians from Cuyens, who went with him to the "Rancheria de Mayem," another 4½ leagues farther on. Then, having forded the river to the east shore, they went still another 2 leagues to a rancheria "que se llama ... Taualames." The Rio Dolores (Tuolumne) was supposed to be 2 to 3 leagues north. However, Viader went upstream on the east bank 6 leagues to the Rio Merced, having in the meantime passed "en frente de ... los indios Apelamenes y Tatives."

The distances on both trips are very consistent and the village locations check closely with those shown on Schenck's map, except that only the Taualames should be placed on the east bank of the river. Viader is very explicit in saying that all the others were on the west bank.

Cuyens, Mayem, and Bozenats are beyond doubt villages, since each was named after its chief, or captain. The Tationes and Apaglamnes are given in the plural: "los indios Apelamenes y Tatives." They may well have possessed more than one rancheria each, as is supposed by Schenck. Schenck thinks that Cuyens and Mayem were transient parties from Kroeber's Miwok villages, Chuyumkatat and Mayemam, which were on the Cosumnes. Aside from the possible similarity in names there is not the slightest evidence in Viader's diaries to support such a theory. Viader definitely specifies rancherias, and the missionaries of that period were able to distinguish rancherias from fishing parties.

From the record we have in this area five villages certain and at least one other probable. For six villages of average size (there is no indication that they were smaller) the population would be assumed as 300 persons each, or 1,800 in all.

The mission records show for baptisms:

| Tribe or Village | Dates of Conversion | Number of Baptisms |
|---|---|---|
| Cuyens | 1811-1813 | 88 |
| Mayemes | 1813-1823 | 91 |
| Apaglamnes | 1818-1824 | 48 |
| Tationes | 1805-1811 | 243 |

The total is 470. These were San Joaquin River natives, not from the delta and marsh region. On the other hand they were less remote from Spanish influence and attack than the tribes which extended up the lateral streams. Hence the proportion of baptisms was probably intermediate between the value of 50 per cent assumed for the very exposed bay and delta people and that of 10 per cent ascribed to the Cosumnes. An estimate of 25 per cent would be reasonable, yielding a population value of 1,800. The two methods of calculation coincide, and the result, 1,800 inhabitants, may be allowed for the area.

For the lower Stanislaus and Tuolumne rivers the only tribes mentioned in the Spanish documents are the Tauhalames (or Taulamnes) on the Tuolumne and the Lakisamne (or Lakisumne or Laquisemne) on the Stanislaus. Kroeber (1925, p. 485) writes: "the Tawalimni, presumably on Tuolumne River ... the Lakisamni ... on the Stanislaus ..." Schenck says (p. 141):

> The villages of Taulamne and Taualames are both definitely placed, the former on an inaccessible rock on the Stanislaus river in the foothills, the latter at the ford of the San Joaquin just below the mouth of the Tuolumne river.... This seems to establish the region between the lower Tuolumne and Stanislaus rivers as Taulamne territory. Merriam agrees in assigning the same region to the Tuolumne.

Schenck's only reference to the Lakisamne is on the same page: "The Leuchas might possibly be identified with Kroeber's Lakisamni (Yokuts) on the Stanislaus river." But the mission records and all other documents clearly distinguish between the two groups, rendering Schenck's hypothesis entirely untenable.

Some of the confusion may derive from the account of Muñoz. In his diary of the Moraga expedition he tells how, on October 1, 1806, the party left the Merced River and proceded northwest for 7 to 8 leagues, reaching finally a river which they called the Dolores (i.e., the Tuolumne, probably near Modesto). There were no Indians, but signs of "varias rancherias," the inhabitants having all absconded. On October 2 they went northwest again and at 4 leagues, in the middle of a very large oak park, they came upon another river, which they called the Guadelupe. This could only have been the Stanislaus, probably somewhere east of Ripon. On the next day, October 3, they went up this river, and at the end of 6 leagues reached a rancheria called Taulamne. It was situated in "unos empinados voladeros e inacesibles por unas encrespadas rocas." They could not get at the Indians but estimated the population as 200, on the basis of the people they could discern. This village, be it noted, was situated among "steep cliffs, inaccessible because of certain rough rocks"—not on an inaccessible rock in the river. This spot, judging by both the distances and the description, was along the limestone bluffs which steeply border the south bank of the Stanislaus for several miles opposite Knights Ferry. The Indians said that there were six other rancherias upstream. From this point the expedition moved the next day again northwest toward the Calaveras River. We gather little concerning tribal names from Moraga's account but we learn that there was a considerable population along the Stanislaus which demonstrated sharp defiance to the Spanish invaders.

In the later documents there is little if any reference to the Taulamnes but much discussion of the Lakisamni. There are repeated allusions to this group as being very hostile, bad raiders, and the object of several military campaigns, particularly those against the great Indian rebel chief, Estanislao. The fighting was undoubtedly on the Stanislaus River and the Indian protagonists were frequently allied with the Cosumnes and Mokelumnes. From the context of the documents they would seem to have been as numerous, or at least as bellicose, as either of these two tribes.

José Sanchez in 1826 refers to his bitter battle with Estanislao, which took place on the "rio de los Laquisimes" (MS, 1826). Joaquin Piña describes a military expedition under Guadelupe Vallejo in 1829 (MS, 1829). The objective was two "rancherias," one of the Laquisimes and the other of the Tagualames, on the "Rio de los Laquisimes," or the "Rio Pescadero." The campaign was inconclusive since nearly all of the Indians escaped.

From the citations above it appears probable that the Taulamnes and the Lakisamne were two distinct tribal groups and that their home was on both the Tuolumne and Stanislaus rivers. It is also likely that in the turmoil and confusion of the period between 1800 and 1830 the original spacing and distribution of the tribes became irreparably lost and that the surviving fragments of both amalgamated and reconstituted themselves with reference to their Spanish enemies rather than with reference to their aboriginal social organization. Hence they may have come to be concentrated more on the Stanislaus than on the Tuolumne.

The only direct population estimate we have for them is that of Muñoz, who claimed 200 persons for the village of Taulamne, among the cliffs. Assuming that 50 persons were not seen, the village would have had 250 inhabitants, which is more or less standard for the general area, according to Moraga's account. If the other six villages had an equal population, the total would have been 1,500. But this estimate does not include the portion of the Stanislaus below Taulamne which was covered by Moraga in his march of 6 leagues upstream. No villages are mentioned in connection with this march but they could scarcely have failed to exist. Hence we may add another 500 without much fear of exaggeration, making a total of 2,000 for the course of the river from the San Joaquin to several miles above Knights Ferry. On the Tuolumne "varias rancherias" were seen, all deserted by their occupants. However, Moraga also remarked that the lower Tuolumne resembled the lower Merced. On the latter were 8 rancherias, hence there may have been an equal number on the Tuolumne. At a conservative 225 persons in each, the aggregate would have been 1,800. The sum for the two rivers would be 3,800.

The baptism lists show 151 conversions for the Lakisamne and 263 for the Taulamnes, or 414 in all. In view of the notorious hostility and the successful resistance these groups opposed to the white men, evident even in Moraga's day, we are justified in setting the baptism factor as low as for the Mokelumnes, or 7 per cent. This gives a potential aboriginal population of 5,920.

The midcentury American estimates would indicate more than this number. H. W. Wessells (1859) claims 500 to 700 on the Stanislaus and Tuolumne in 1853. Adam Johnston (1853) put 1,350 on his map of the same area in 1852. W. M. Ryer vaccinated 1,010 on the two rivers in 1851. The Daily Alta California for May 31, 1851, said that the Indians were 1,000 strong between the Stanislaus and the Tuolumne, and Savage, for an earlier period, put them at 4,600 (Dixon, MS, 1875). On the other hand, it must be remembered that as a result of Spanish and Mexican, not to mention American, aggression most of the strictly San Joaquin River people had long since retreated up the lateral streams. Hence the natives seen by the commissioners between 1850 and 1853 included the residues of all the river tribes from Manteca to Merced. For the southern part of the San Joaquin Valley it was determined, in a previous discussion, that the population remainder in 1850 represented approximately one-third of the aboriginal population. Of the estimates just cited the most reliable is that of Ryer. Following the suggestions presented in the consideration of his activities, we must make a correction to account for persons who missed vaccination. Such a correction would bring the number to 1,420. Then application of the factor one-third gives an aboriginal value of 4,730.

The three modes of estimate yield respectively a population of 3,800, 5,920, and 4,730, with an average of 4,817. We may use a slightly greater value and call the population 5,000. To this must be added the 1,800 persons estimated to have lived along the San Joaquin River itself. The lower San Joaquin River group as a whole, therefore, may be assigned a population of 6,800.

Lower San Joaquin River Group ... 6,800

NORTHERN SAN JOAQUIN VALLEY ... 27,070

## THE MIWOK FOOTHILL AREA

Above the central valley itself and occupying the foothills from the Cosumnes to the Tuolumne lived the northern and central Miwok. This region was not reached by the Spanish expeditions nor were many, if any, of the inhabitants incorporated in the missions. It is therefore necessary to rely exclusively upon the reports of the ethnographers. In a preceding discussion of the central Miwok, who lived on the upper Stanislaus and Tuolumne, there were cited the data secured by Gifford, Kroeber, and Merriam for 70 villages. This area in 1850 was estimated to contain a population of 1,470. There are no data comparable to Gifford's for the rivers farther north, largely because the natives on the upper Cosumnes, Mokelumne, and Calaveras were thoroughly dispersed during the Gold Rush and village names and locations have become lost to the memory of Indian and white man alike. It is possible, however, to get a reasonable estimate of the population indirectly.

The territory of the northern Miwok, from the ecological standpoint resembles closely that of the central Miwok. Hence stream mileage and area comparisons are justified. If we use the boundaries of the two groups substantially as given by Kroeber in the Handbook (map, opp. p. 446) and plot rivers and areas on a large-scale map, the equivalent aboriginal population for the northern Miwok by stream mileage and area is 2,480 and 1,535, respectively. The discrepancy in the two estimates is due to the greater frequency of streams and creeks in the northern area. The average of the population calculated by the two methods is 2,008, very close to that found for the central Miwok. The total for the foothill strip is then 4,138 or in round numbers 4,150.

MIWOK FOOTHILL AREA ... 4,150

## FOOTNOTES:

[5] There are numerous other letters pertaining to this matter in the same volume of the Provincial State Papers.

# SUMMARY AND CONCLUSIONS

From the data presented in detail in the last section we may now derive the aboriginal population of the San Joaquin Valley as a whole.

| Region | | Population |
|---|---|---|
| Tulare Lake Basin | | 6,500 |
| Kaweah River | | 7,600 |
| Merced River | | 3,500 |
| Kings River | | 9,100 |
| Mariposa, Fresno, Chowchilla, upper San Joaquin | | 19,000 |
| Southern San Joaquin Valley | | 6,900 |
| Northern San Joaquin Valley | | |
| Delta area | 9,350 | |
| Lower Cosumnes | 5,200 | |
| Lower Mokelumne | 5,720 | |
| Lower San Joaquin, Calaveras, Tuolumne, and Stanislaus | 6,800 | 27,070 |
| Foothill strip (central and northern Miwok) | | 4,150 |
| Total | | 83,820 |

The total, 83,820, is more than four times as large as the population estimated to be surviving in 1850 (19,000) and much exceeds any previous estimate advanced by modern students of the California Indians.

Dr. C. Hart Merriam in 1905 computed the population of the entire state of California as 260,000, of whom perhaps one-fifth may have occupied the San Joaquin Valley, although Merriam does not attempt to assess the population of this area as such. Kroeber discusses the matter at length in the Handbook (pp. 488-491, 880-891) and concludes that the population of the whole state was 133,000. Of these the Yokuts had 18,000, the Miwok (Plains and Sierra) 9,000, the Western Mono about 1,000, and the peripheral tribes in the south perhaps 2,000, a total of 30,000. Schenck is more liberal, since for the delta region he allows for a spread of between 3,000 and 15,000 persons. The present estimate for the same area, as closely as it can be determined, is in the vicinity of 13,000, or within Schenck's limits although toward his upper extreme.

Since the data and reasoning upon which the present figure of 83,820 is based are set forth in detail in the preceding pages there is little value in repeating them, nor will anything be gained by attempting a rebuttal to the arguments presented by Kroeber. At the same time the author may be permitted to recapitulate three points wherein he thinks many modern scholars have been misled.

1. All available information from the Spanish and Mexican sources must be consulted. To confine an argument or an estimate to a single account, such as that by Moraga, may lead to a false impression. Kroeber seems to have been thus deceived in his discussion of the population of the Yokuts.

2. It must be remembered that in the central valley, as contrasted perhaps with an area like the Klamath River, no informants speaking since 1900, and particularly since 1920, can possibly have furnished a true picture of conditions prior to the Spanish invasion in the decade following 1800.

3. The depletion of population in the San Joaquin Valley between 1800 and 1850 was far greater than has been appreciated, although the basic facts have always been recognized. Warfare, massacre, forced conversion, starvation, and exposure all took a tremendous toll of life but the sweeping epidemics of the 1830's were even more devastating. Together these forces destroyed in the aggregate fully 75 per cent of the aboriginal population.

# APPENDIX

After this manuscript was completed, the writer had an opportunity to examine those documentary files of the Office of Indian Affairs and of the War Department which are at present in the National Archives at Washington. Several letters in the files containing information on the native population of the San Joaquin Valley have never, so far as could be determined, been published. Since the data thus procured are fragmentary and since they do not apparently invalidate the conclusions set forth in previous pages, they have not been incorporated in the body of this paper. These items, however, have some intrinsic interest and therefore merit specific mention. They are briefly abstracted as follows.

<u>War Department</u>

<u>Record Group 98.</u> 10th Military Dept. Letters received Calif., Document no. <u>K 21</u>. E. D. Keyes, Camp Magruder, June 17, 1851.

The 8 tribes on the Kaweah, with whom a treaty was concluded on May 30 contain 1,240 individuals.

The 4 tribes on Paint Creek with whom a treaty was concluded on June 3 contain 1,660 persons.

<u>Record Group 98.</u> Letters received Calif., 1854. Enclosure to document no. <u>W 2.</u> John Nugent, Camp Wessells, Dec. 31, 1853.

The Four Creeks region (Kaweah) from the Sierra Nevada to Tulare Lake will not contain more than 1,000, all told.

<u>Record Group 98.</u> Letters received Calif., 1854. Enclosure to document no. <u>W 12.</u> H. W. Wessells, Fort Miller, March 7, 1854.

The Indians under control of Fort Miller include those on the Fresno, San Joaquin, Kings, and Kaweah Rivers. They are much reduced in numbers, owing to the recent sickness.

Fresno River: 400 persons, including 100 able men.

San Joaquin River: 350, including 80-90 able men.

Kings River: 1,100, including 250 able men.

Kaweah River: 800, including 200 able men.

Office of Indian Affairs

Record Group 75. Letters received Calif., 1854. Enclosure to document no. H 758. D. A. Enyart, Fresno Reservation, Nov. 3, 1854.

The Indians on the Fresno Farm include: 30 Chowchilla, 220 Choot-chances, 90 Pohonicha, and 100 Potohanchi.

The Indians in Mariposa, Stanislaus, and Tuolumne counties do not exceed a total of 2,000.

By river system he breaks them down thus: 300 on the Merced, 350 on the Tuolumne, 250 at Plant's Ferry on the Stanislaus, 100 elsewhere on the Stanislaus, and 100 scattering through the country.

Record Group 75. Letters received Calif., 1855. Enclosure to document no. H 1050. Report of D. A. Enyart, Fresno Reservation, Aug. 22, 1855.

"I find that there are at least about 1,000 to 1,500 Indians on the River (i.e., San Joaquin).... This does not include the 'Mono' tribe which is the most numerous of any tribe...."

Record Group 75. Letters received Calif., 1859. Enclosure to document no. M 66. M. B. Lewis, Fresno Agency, Aug. 30, 1859.

A report on the 22 tribes which recognize the Fresno Agency as their headquarters. Abstracted as follows:

Wel-leelch-um-nies:
the most northerly tribe; is "temporarily" on the Tuolumne
River because of displacement by the whites.                    85

Poto-en-cies:
have abandoned their native land, the Merced
Valley and are now on the Chowchilla.                           110

Noot-choos:
"a union of the remnant of other tribes," including some
Yosemites. Now on the north fork of the Chowchilla.             85

Po-ho-nee-chees:
on the headwaters of the Fresno.                                        105

Chow-chillas:
have moved from the Chowchilla to the Fresno River.                     85

Cooc-chances:
the largest "unbroken" tribe in the agency, originally on
Coarse Gold Creek; some still there, some at agency.                    240

How-ches:
once large; always have been on the Fresno.                             18

Pit-cat-ches and Tal-linches:
(two distinct tribes); native habitat was the San
Joaquin River; still near Fort Miller.                                  150

Coss-waz:
"to some extent identified with the Pit-cat-
ches"; native land is Deer Creek.                                       88

Monos:
on Fine Gold Creek and the upper San Joaquin River.                     535

War-to-kes, Itee-ches, and Cho-pes:
all on Kings River; "constitute one nation" but
have separate heads (on Wartoke Creek).                                 290

Wat-ches:
since 1854 have been on Kings River Farm.                               75

No-to-no-tos and We-melches.                                            190

Tat-ches and Wo-wells:
these four tribes are native to the lower Kings
River and Tulare Lake. They were recently                               165
driven to their homes on the Fresno Farm.

Cow-willas:
their home is the mouth of the Kaweah at the foothills.                 110

Tel-em-nies:
on the Kaweah, near Visalia.                                            105

                                                                        — —

Total                                                                   2,436

# BIBLIOGRAPHY

## PUBLISHED WORKS


Barbour, G. W.

1852. 32nd Cong., 1st sess., Sen. Ex. Doc. 1, pt. III.

1853. Report to the Indian Commissioner. 33rd Cong., spec. sess., Sen. Ex. Doc. 4, pp. 249-264 [Ser. no. 688].

Barbour, G. W., R. McKee, and O. M. Wozencraft

1853. Report to the Indian Commissioner. 33rd Cong., spec. sess., Sen. Ex. Doc. 4, pp. 56-59.

Carson, James H.

1852. In San Joaquin Republican (Stockton, Feb., 1852), as quoted by S. P. Elias, Stories of Stanislaus (Modesto, 1924), p. 196.

Chapman, Charles E.

1911. Expedition on the Sacramento and San Joaquin Rivers in 1817, Diary of Fray Narciso Duran. Publ. Acad. Pacific Coast Hist., Vol. 2, No. 5.

Cook, S. F.

1940. Population Trends among the California Mission Indians. Univ. Calif. Ibero-Americana 17. Berkeley.

Coues, Elliott, ed.

1900. On the Trail of a Spanish Pioneer. (The diary of Francisco Garcés.) Trans, and ed. by Elliott Coues. New York. The parts pertaining to the San Joaquin Valley are in 1:281-300.

Derby, Lt. George H.

1852. A Report of the Tulare Valley. 32nd. Cong., 1st sess., Sen. Ex. Doc. 110, pp. 4-16.

Farquhar, Francis P.

1932. The Topographical Reports of George H. Derby, California Hist. Soc. Quarterly, 11:99, 247, 365.

Gayton, A. H.

1948. Yokuts and Western Mono Ethnography. Univ. Calif. Publ. Anthro. Rec., Vol. 10. Berkeley.

Gifford, E. W.

1932. The Northfork Mono. Univ. Calif. Publ. Am. Arch. and Ethn., 31:15-65. Berkeley.

Gifford, E. W., and W. Egbert Schenck

1926. Archaeology of the Southern San Joaquin Valley, California. Univ. Calif. Publ. Am. Arch. and Ethn., 23:1-122. Berkeley.

Gilbert, F. T.

1879. History of San Joaquin County, California. Oakland, Calif.

Henley, T. J.

1857. Report to the Commissioner of Indian Affairs, accompanying Ann. Rept. Sec. of the Interior for 1856. No. 100, pp. 236-246.

Johnston, Adam

1853. Report to the Indian Commissioner. 33rd Cong., spec. sess., Sen. Ex. Doc. 4, pp. 241-247.

1860. In H. R. Schoolcraft, Archives of Aboriginal Knowledge, 4:406 ff.

Kroeber, A. L.

1925. Handbook of the Indians of California. Bur. Amer. Ethn. Bull. 78. Washington, D. C.

Latta, F. F.

1949. Handbook of Yokuts Indians. Bakersfield, Calif.

Mason, J. D.

1881. History of Amador County, California. Oakland, Calif.

Merriam, C. Hart

1905. The Indian Population of California, American Anthropologist, n.s., 7:594-606.

1907. Distribution and Classification of the Mewan Stock of California, American Anthropologist, n.s., 9:338-357.

Powers, Stephen

1877. Tribes of California, Contributions to North American Ethnology. Washington, D. C.

Ryer, W. M.

1852. Vouchers for vaccination. 32nd Cong., 2nd sess., Sen. Ex. Doc. 61, pp. 20-23 [Ser. no. 620].

Savage, James D.

1851. Letter in the True Standard, reprinted in the Sacramento Union, Apr. 10, 1851.

Schenck, W. Egbert

1926. Historic Aboriginal Groups of the California Delta Region. Univ. Calif. Publ. Am. Arch. and Ethn., 23:123-146. Berkeley.

Sutter, John A.

1850. Letter to H. W. Halleck, Dec. 20, 1847. 31st Cong., 1st sess., H. R. Ex. Doc. 17.

1939. New Helvetia Diary; a Record of Events Kept by John A. Sutter and His Clerks at New Helvetia, California, from September 9, 1845, to May 25, 1848. San Francisco, Calif.

Tinkham, George H.

1923. History of San Joaquin County, California. Los Angeles, Calif.

United States Treaties

1905. Message from the President ... communicating Eighteen Treaties made with Indians in California ... [1851-1852, by G. W. Barbour, O. M. Wozencraft, and Redick McKee.] 32nd Cong., 1st sess., Sen. Con. Doc. Reprint of 1905. Washington, D. C.

Warner, J. J.

Description of 1832 Epidemic among the Indians of the San Joaquin Valley. In An Illustrated History of San Joaquin County, California ... pp. 28-29. The Lewis Publishing Co. Chicago.

Wessels, H. W.

1857. Report on the Tribes of the San Joaquin Valley. 34th Cong., 3rd sess., H. R. Ex. Doc. 76, pp. 31-32.

Wozencraft, O. M.

1851. Letter dated July 12, 1851. 32nd Cong., 1st sess., Sen. Ex. Doc. 1, pt. III, pp. 488-490 [Ser. no. 906].

# MANUSCRIPTS

All manuscripts are in the Bancroft Library, University of California, Berkeley, unless otherwise stated.

Abella, Ramon

Diario de un registro de los Rios Grandes, Oct. 31, 1811, San Francisco. Santa Barbara Archive, IV:101-134. Also original manuscript.

Altimira, José

Letter to Prefect José Senan, July 10, 1823, San Francisco. Archbishop's Archive, IV (2):21-26.

Amador, José Maria

Memorias sobre la Historia de California, 1877. Original manuscript C-D 28.

Argüello, José

Letter to Governor Arrillaga, May 30, 1805, San Francisco. Provincial State Papers, XIX:42 ff.

Argüello, Luís Antonio

Letter to Governor Arrillaga, Oct. 31, 1813, San Francisco. Provincial State Papers, XIX:345-349.

Carta al Gobernador Don Pablo Vicente de Sola ... May 26, 1817, San Francisco. Original manuscript (no. fm F864A64); also typed copy.

Berryesa, José

Dated July 15, 1830, San Jose. Departmental State Papers, II:135-137.

Cabot, Juan

Expedicion al valle de los Tulares, Letter to the Padre Presidente, Apr. 7, 1815. Santa Barbara Archive, VI:67-72.

Letter to De La Guerra, May 23, 1818. De La Guerra Documents, VII:88.

Dixon, H.

California Indians. 1875.

Duran, Narciso

Diario de la expedicion de reconocimiento hecha en el mes de Mayo de 1817.... Original manuscript. (See also Charles E. Chapman, 1911.)

Estudillo, José Maria

Diario que formo yo el tente dn Jose Maria Estudillo en la campaña ... emprendo pa el reconocimiento y visita de las rancherias situadas en los tulares ... Nov. 10, 1819, Monterey. Original manuscript; also typed copy.

Garcia, Inocente

Hechos Historicos de California, 1878. Original manuscript. CC-D 84.

Jaime, Antonio

Letter to Governor Sola, March 30, 1816, Soledad. Archbishop's Archive, III(1):23-24.

Marquinez, Marcelino

Letter to Governor Sola, May 26, 1816. Archbishop's Archive, III(1):41-42.

Martin, Juan

Visita a los Gentiles Tulareños, Apr. 26, 1815, San Miguel. Santa Barbara Archive, VI:85-89.

Martinez, Luís Antonio

Entrada en las Rancherias del Tular, May 29, 1816, San Luis Obispo. Archbishop's Archive, III(1):42-45.

McKinstry, George

Documents for the History of California, 1846-9. Presented by Dr. George McKinstry of San Diego, 1872.

Merriam, C. Hart

Manuscript collection in Department of Anthropology, University of California, Berkeley.

Moraga, Gabriel

Diario de la tercera expedicion echa por el Alferez Don Gabriel Moraga ... a los rios del norte; verificada en el mes de septiembre de el año de 1808. Original manuscript; also two typed copies.

Muñoz, Pedro

Diario de la Expn echa por D. Gabriel Moraga de la Compania de San Francisco a los nuevos descubrimientos del tular ... Nov. 2, 1806, San Francisco. Santa Barbara Archive, IV:1-47.

Ortega, Juan de

Diario que forma el Sargto Distdo Dn Juan de Ortega segun los sitios qe por orn. del Sr. Govor de su mando registrar ... Dec. 2, 1815, San Juan Bautista. Original manuscript; also typed copy.

Pico, José Dolores

Diario formado pr el Sargto José Dolores Pico de la expedicion que a echo pr dispocion del ciudadano ... José Estudillo, Jan. 31, 1826. Original manuscript.

Piña, Joaquin

Quaderno de las Novedades Hoccuridas diariamente en la expedicion que marcha a las ordenes del ... Guadelupe Vallejo, June 13, 1829, Monterey. Original manuscript; also a copy in the California Manuscript series, no. E-88.

Rodriguez, Sebastián

Diario que forma yo el Sargto Sebastian Rodriguez de la Campana nombrada el dia 17 de Abril de 1828 [dated May 8, 1828]. Original manuscript.

Diario formado pr el Sargento Sebastian Rodriguez desde el dia 26 de Mayo ... una expedicion al Tular por el rumbo de S. Miguel, June 22, 1828, Monterey. Manuscript.

Sal, Hermenegildo

... Informe en el cual el teniente Hermdo Sal manifesta lo que ha adquirido de varios sugetos para comunicarlo al Governador dela Provincia; Jan. 31, 1796. Provincial State Papers, XIV:14-16.

Sanchez, José

Letter to Ignacio Martinez, May 10, 1826. State Papers, Missions and Colonization, II:15-20.

Savage, James

In H. Dixon, California Indians. MS 1875.

Viader, José

Diario, o noticia del viaje que acabo de hacer ... desde el 15 hasta el 28 de Agosto de 1810, Aug. 28, 1910, San Juan Bautista. Santa Barbara Archive, IV:73-84.

Diario del P. Jose desde 19 hasta 27 de Octubre de 1810. Letter to the Padre Presidente, Oct. 19, 1810, San Jose. Santa Barbara Archive, IV:85-94.

Zalvidea, José Maria

Diario de una expedicion tierra adentro, 1806. Santa Barbara Archive, IV:49-68.

[TN: Click on maps for larger views.]

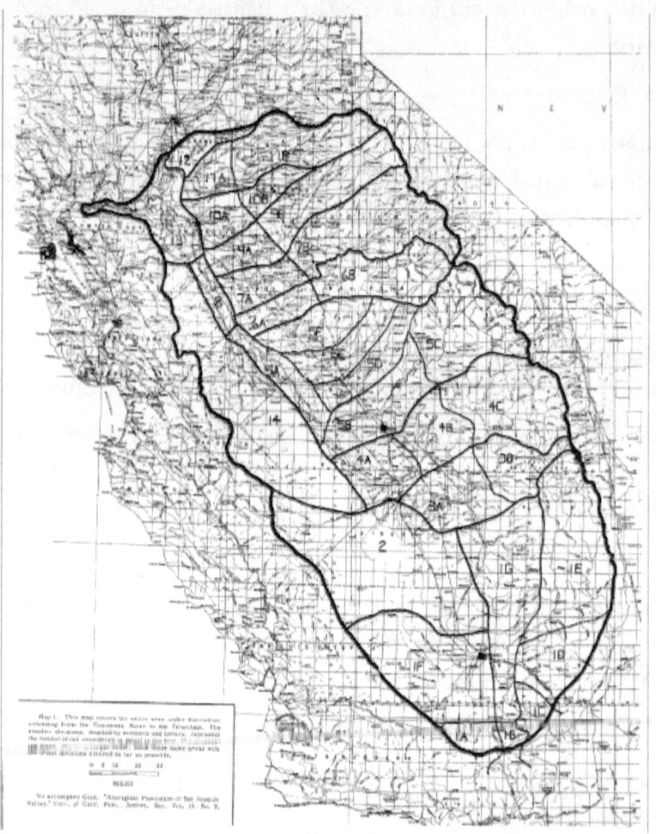

**Map 1. This map covers the entire area under discussion, extending from the Cosumnes River to the Tehachapi. The smaller divisions, denoted by numbers and letters, represent the habitat areas considered in detail in the text. The succeeding maps, drawn to larger scale, show these same areas with the tribal divisions entered as far as possible.**

**To accompany Cook, "Aboriginal Population of San Joaquin Valley," Univ. of Calif. Publ., Anthro. Rec. Vol. 16, No. 2.**

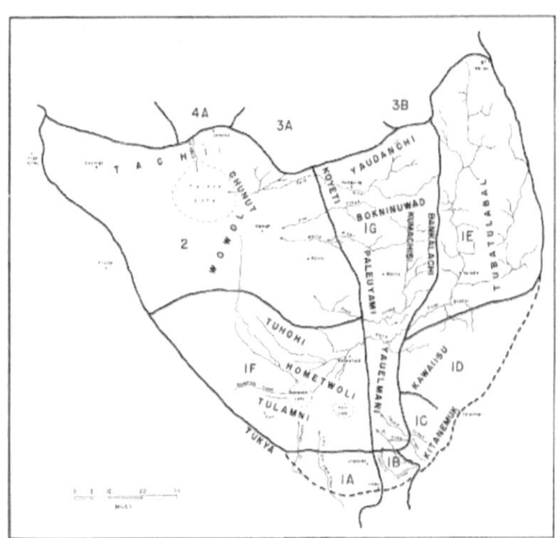

Map 2. Habitat areas 1A-2: the southern Yokuts and peripheral tribes.

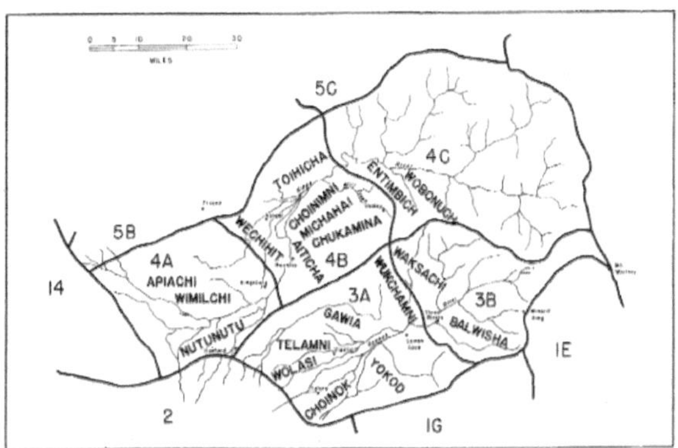

Map 3. Habitat areas 3A-4C: the basins of the Kaweah and
Kings rivers, including the Yokuts and part of the Mono.

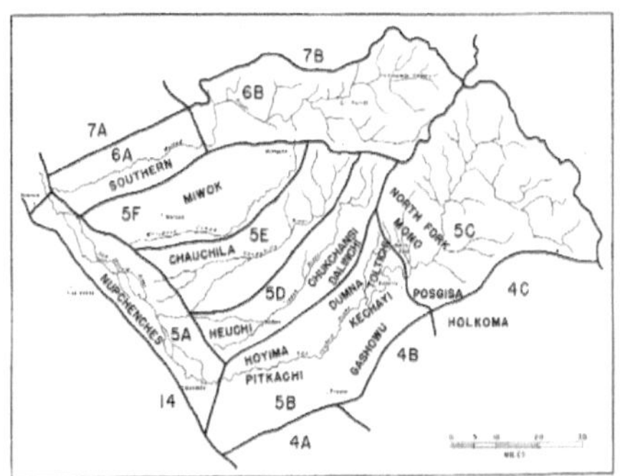

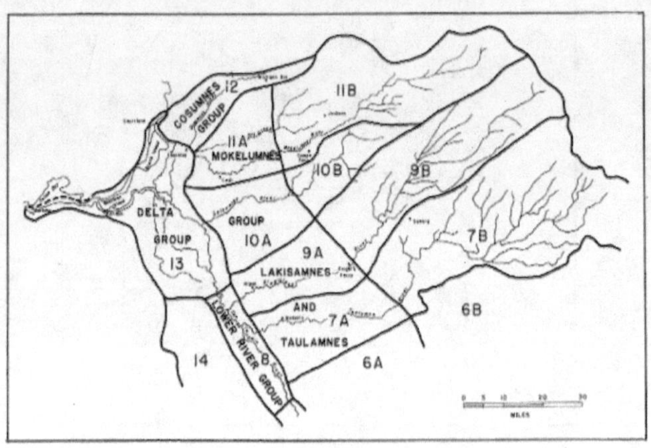

Map 5. Habitat areas 7A-14: the Northern Yokuts,
Central and Northern Miwok.

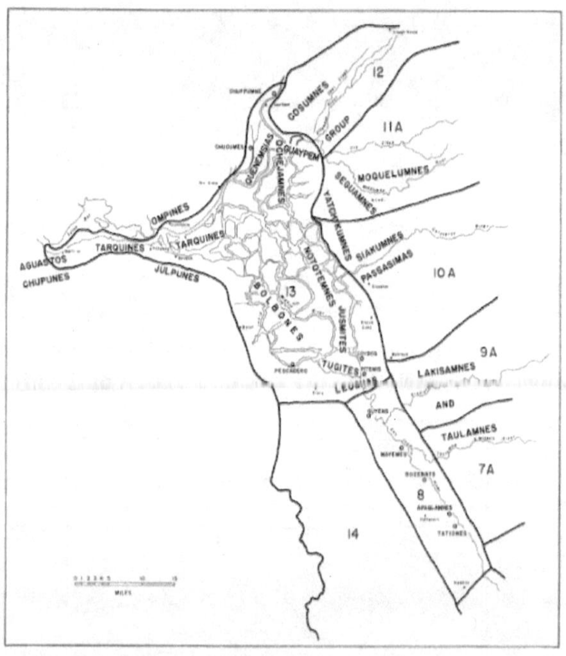

Map 6. The Lower San Joaquin River and Delta
areas (particularly areas 8 and 13).